LECTIONARY STORIES, CYCLE A

40 Tellable Tales For Advent, Christmas,
Epiphany, Lent, Easter And Pentecost

BY JOHN E. SUMWALT

C.S.S. Publishing Co., Inc.
Lima, Ohio

All characters and events in this collection are fictitious except for those in the stories titled "Carrying The Cross," "Opening The Scriptures," "When Peace Came," "Almost In Heaven," "Steve's Call," "Close Call," "Between A Rock And A Hard Place," "In A Land of Deep Darkness," and "Through The Ice," one of the stories in the sermon titled "Who May Come To The Banquet?"

Library of Congress Cataloging-in-Publication Data

Sumwalt, John E.
　　Lectionary stories. Cycle A : 40 tellable tales for Advent, Christmas, Epiphany, Lent, Easter and Pentecost / by John E. Sumwalt.
　　　　p.　　cm.
　　ISBN 1-55673-436-0
　　i. Homiletical illustrations. 2. Common lectionary. 3. Bible — Homiletical use.
I. Title.
BV4225.2.S954　　1992
251'.08—dc20　　　　　　　　　　　　　　　　　　　　　92-10855
　　　　　　　　　　　　　　　　　　　　　　　　　　　　CIP

9239 / ISBN 1-55673-436-0　　　　　　　　　　PRINTED IN U.S.A.

To my wife, Jo, without
whose love and technical
support this book would
not have been possible.

Contents

Afterword

Foreword

On our third date in 1975, my wife Jo and I attended a Guthrie Theater road production which included excerpts from several contemporary plays. I don't remember anything about the plays or the actors except that they were much better than the local amateurs I was used to seeing. But I do recall that afterwards, on the way to her parents' house, as we discussed what we had seen, I discovered that Jo shared my interest in writing. I was writing poetry in those days and had attempted a few short stories. Jo had written several stories while in high school, and, what impressed me most, a script for the television series *Bonanza,* which she never sent to NBC. I told her about the book I had started at the age of 12, and she described the novel she was planning in her mind. We both dreamed of writing for publication one day. It was in that moment that I began to fall in love with Jo. The rest, as they say, is history. We were married within six months. Now, 17 years, two children, and two academic degrees (one for her and one for me) later, our dream is beginning to come true.

It has been a great joy to collaborate on these 40 *Lectionary Stories For Cycle A*. Jo served as a silent, less active partner on my first two books, *Lectionary Stories For Cycles B and C*, correcting my inept attempts at punctuation and challenging me when a story needed more work (although I didn't always listen). I owe much of the success of these books to her expert technical guidance, emotional support and inspiration.

When Jo completed her degree work recently, we decided to enter into a full writing partnership. She has edited most of the stories in this volume and authored "Past Glory," "One More Time," "Last Words" and "A Pretty Little Room."

We are grateful to Kenneth Lyerly for sharing his three personal stories: "Carrying The Cross," "Opening The

Scriptures," and "When Peace Came;" to Stephen Groves for the story of his call to pastoral ministry; to my father A. Leonard Sumwalt for the story of his close call; and to Robert and Lillian Vohland for allowing us to share the story of their daughter, Jessica.

Our special thanks to Morris and Leta Vinz, Wesley and Brenda White, Lloyd Lewis, Frank Gaylord, Tom Garnhart, Joyce Alford, David Lawson, Mary Hicks Good, Jeffrey Nicholas, Darnell Mason, Florence Schieber and Ernest Vohland for critiquing selected stories.

John E. Sumwalt

How I Prepare To Preach

I begin to prepare for preaching by reading the biblical text a few times. When I am grasped by the word in some way, I formulate a theme. Sometimes the title and the whole thrust of the sermon will come to me at once. Then I label a folder and add thoughts, newspaper clippings, quotations from movies, plays, novels and illustrations that occur to me as the weeks go by. I always gather more material than I can use.

Sometimes I do the exegetical work and word study on several texts weeks in advance, but more often I do it on the Tuesday morning of the week I am going to preach. This process usually gives me several idea bursts, which I jot down in the oral form in which I have learned to think and write sermons, saying some phrases and thoughts aloud as I go. About mid-morning I prepare the order of worship, paying close attention to the content of the liturgy, especially the hymns, and asking myself how the whole service flows from the text.

I share my sermon ideas with a lectionary study group that meets on Tuesday afternoons. We discuss such questions as: What is the word for us in this text? What is the word for the people of our congregations? What can we say that will help them hear the word? What might their reactions be? What can we say that they haven't heard before?

Then the real work begins. I start to preach the sermon in my mind as I jog in the morning or as I'm taking a shower or preparing a meal. It is in my consciousness in almost every spare moment. I carry on a continuous dialogue with those I imagine will be present in worship, asking myself how this word will be heard. The struggles, sorrows, hurts and staunch beliefs of certain individuals come to mind, and my conversation (sermon) is shaped accordingly. Much of this happens intuitively. The subconscious part of the process may be as

11

important as what happens consciously. I frequently get up in the middle of the night to write down a thought or an idea from a dream that I'm afraid might be lost if I wait until morning.

I am often heard mumbling in the study and seen gesturing and grimacing as I drive the car on these days between Tuesday and Friday. I am irritable and forgetful. My family and friends have learned to identify this disease as PPS syndrome (Preaching Preparation Syndrome). There is no known cure.

I put the sermon in the final written form on Friday morning, then let it rest until Saturday afternoon when I read, think and speak through it again. I pencil in new ideas and delete material that seems unnecessary. This process is repeated early on Sunday morning, before I jog. Any further adjustments to the sermon text are made mostly in my mind up until the time I start to preach. Many changes, deletions and additions are made as I speak to the congregation and respond to the feedback that I receive during the preaching moment.

Sometimes as I study and ponder the scripture, a story will come to me which I will share as a part of the sermon. This usually occurs when it becomes clear that just explaining or illustrating an idea will not carry the meaning of the text. Much of the Bible is narrative. Stories are woven together in a certain order to enable the hearers of the word to enter into the presence of God. Gabriel Josipovici writes in *The Book of God: A Response To The Bible,* in recent years more and more theologians ". . . have begun to show a new interest in story and poetry, and even to argue that a significant aspect of God's message is that it should be delivered as story and poem, and that we cannot understand it at all unless we accept this fact."[1] Most modern preachers only comment on these narratives, thereby objectifying them: an act which distances both the commentators and the rest of the worshiping community from the presence of God in the word. Telling a story inspired by scripture serves the double function of commenting on the text and allowing the hearer to attend to God's presence in both the old (the scripture) and the new narrative (the sermon).

I share created stories in about four out of 10 sermons. These are inspired by memories, dreams and my imagination, as well as the biblical texts. This is a work I do intentionally, although a few of what I consider to be my best stories have come to me as a gift of the spirit, without any apparent intellectual effort on my part. These kinds of stories come to me whole. I know in a single inspiration how they will begin and end. Usually, though, story creating is difficult, painstaking — albeit joyful — work, which begins for me with a theological or moral problem. I create a character or characters and place them in a setting where they will be required to deal with the problem suggested by the text. As the characters interact with one another and with God and the narrative unfolds, I am often surprised at the outcome. The creative process has an inherent integrity which does not allow me to contrive a conclusion for my own homiletical purposes.

There are some weeks (more than I care to remember) when the agony of preparation is excruciating: when none of the disciplines I have cultivated over the years are helpful. The sermon, like a baby born breach, comes slowly, painfully and in its own time, or perhaps God's own time. It is in such moments that I curse my calling and wish that I had never been born, or at least that I had chosen another profession. Still, I have found that if I am faithful in telling the story, God will deliver a word that is alive and life-giving, in spite of me and all of my efforts to be a good preacher.

---

[1]Gabriel Josipovici, *The Book Of God: A Response To The Bible* (New Haven: Yale UP, 1988) xii.

Come, Lord Jesus

*Then two will be in the field; one will be taken and
the other left. Two women will be grinding meal
together; one will be taken and the other left. Keep
awake therefore, for you do not know on what day
your Lord is coming.*

Matthew 24:41-42

Two women lay in their beds on the third floor of a downtown nursing home. They have been roommates for many
years. One is 105 years old and the other is 102. They have
been waiting and watching for a long, long time. "It won't
be long now," they assure one another at the beginning of each
new day. "It can't be much longer now." And every night,
when the lights go out, they close their eyes and pray, "Come
soon, Lord Jesus, come soon."

One morning, just before dawn, one of the women is
wakened by a strange, floating sensation. When she opens her
eyes, she is surprised to find herself near the ceiling of the room,
looking down at the still form of her own body on the bed
below. Across the room she can see the blanket which covers
her roommate heaving up and down with each labored breath.
She notices for the first time how old and tired her friend appears there in the bed which has been her home for so many
years. She waits for a moment, thinking her friend might be
coming, too. And then, knowing she can wait no longer, she
blows her a kiss and turns to greet the dawn.

14

The Wrath To Come

Then the people of Jerusalem and all Judea were going out to him, and all the region along the Jordan, and they were baptized by him in the river Jordan, confessing their sins. But when he saw many Pharisees and Sadducees coming for baptism, he said to them, "You brood of vipers! Who warned you to flee from the wrath to come?"

Matthew 3:5-7

He went very much unnoticed at first: a solitary voice sounding off on the high-numbered cable channels late at night, when air time was cheap. "There was a time," he always began, "when we lived in a world of unlimited resources and great beauty; we breathed unfiltered air and drank unprocessed water straight from streams and wells. Fresh fruit and vegetables were shipped directly from the field to the market. There were no poison control centers, no radioactive islands, no mutant cities fenced off for the genetically deformed. Our ancestors walked outside without breathing devices or sun-protective clothing. They could see the stars and moon at night, and they required no special operations to enable them to reproduce. Now we are a dying race clinging to a decaying planet: the last generation to live on the earth. It will not be long now. The time is short. The new world may come at any moment. It could come tomorrow; it may be next month or next year. It may happen yet tonight, before the sun rises on another day."

It was at this point that he always held up the two-litre plastic bottle of pure, artesian spring water pumped directly, he said, from virgin springs in underground caverns deep in the earth. No one outside his small circle of disciples and

15

employees knew for sure where the water came from, but it was widely reported that it had healing and restorative powers. The camera zoomed in close so the viewers could read the large, blue letters scrawled in a bold cursive script full-length across the label: Maranatha, it read in ancient Greek. Printed beneath in smaller, red letters were translations into several world languages — French, Russian, German, Spanish, Chinese, Korean and English — "Our Lord Come."

"Act now to purify your body and soul," he said. "You can be among the thousands and thousands who have already prepared themselves for the coming new world." Then, as the 800 number appeared on the screen along with the price of the water, his voice would become softer and softer as he invited everyone to call now, because tomorrow might be too late.

He became known as the Pure Water Prophet. Orders came in from all around the world. He sent plane loads and ship loads of his special water to nearly every city in every nation. The clergy and lay leaders of all of the major denominations condemned him at first. But after the great earthquake in 2034 that shook every continent and killed over a hundred million people, many of them called asking if they could become purified believers, too. But he would not fill their orders. He always saved his most scathing rebukes for them near the end of the program. "You pampered snakes," he said, "living in comfort in your antiseptic cathedrals while the poor are poisoned in the streets. Who told you to flee from the wrath to come?"

Patient Waiting

Be patient, therefore, beloved, until the coming of the Lord. The farmer waits for the precious crop from the earth, being patient with it until it receives the early and late rains. You also must be patient. Strengthen your hearts, for the coming of the Lord is near.

James 5:7-8

Herb Minton stepped into the whirlpool at the YMCA where several of his friends were already soaking in the hot, steamy water and conversing, as men do, about the deep, ultimate, existential concerns of *man*kind — like the point spread on the coming Monday night football game, the ridiculously high salaries of professional baseball players (they were about evenly divided on that one), and the price of American cars compared to German and Japanese models. The conversation flowed from one topic to another — family matters, how difficult it is to raise kids today, high taxes, national politics, local gossip, the differences between men and women — till finally they got to talking about human nature. That was when the conversation became quite heated, almost as hot as the water. One man expressed very loudly, and in language he wouldn't have used in church, that most people he knew only looked out for themselves. "When it comes right down to it," he said, "we are all basically selfish. Take care of number one and to heck with everyone else."

That was when Herb pulled himself up out of the water to cool off, and said in a quiet voice, "I don't agree with you, and I'll tell you why. I saw something recently that I have not been able to get out of my mind. As you all know, I am a jogger. Every afternoon, when I get off work at the plant, I jog

17

about a mile and a half to the convenience store on the corner to pick up my daily paper, and then I turn around and jog home. I run slowly, so it is enough to keep my heart aerobically fit.

"One day when I went into the store, the man behind the counter who saves my paper for me, and whom I've known for years, was standing at the window with tears in his eyes, staring out at the bus stop across the street. He turned to me after a bit and said, 'Herb, do you see that bench over there?' I nodded and he went on. 'There's an old woman who comes there every day around this time. She sits there for about an hour, knitting and waiting. Buses come and go, but she never boards one and she never meets anyone who is getting off. She just knits and waits. I took a cup of coffee over to her one day and sat with her for a while. She told me that her son is in the Navy. She last saw him two years ago when he left town on one of the buses right out there. He's married now, and he and his wife have a baby daughter. The woman has never met her daughter-in-law or seen her grandchild, and they're the only family she has. She told me, "It helps to come here and wait. I pray for them as I knit little things for the baby, and I imagine them in their tiny apartment on the base. They are saving money to come home on the bus next Christmas. I can't wait to see them." '

"My friend behind the counter took a deep breath and then he said, 'I looked out there just now, and there they were getting off the bus. You should have seen the look on her face when they fell into her arms, and when she laid eyes on her little granddaughter for the first time. It was the nearest thing to pure joy that I ever hope to see. I'll never forget that look for as long as I live.' "

Herb sat down in the hot water again and paused for a moment before he said, "When I went back the next day my friend was in his usual place behind the counter. Before he could say anything, or even hand me my paper, I looked him in the eye and I said to him, 'You sent her son the money for the bus tickets, didn't you?' He looked at me with eyes full of love

18

and a smile that was the nearest thing to complete joy that I have ever seen, and said, 'Yes, I sent him the money.'

"I'll never forget that look for as long as I live."

It was quiet in the whirlpool for a long time after that. No one wanted to be the first to speak.

A Righteous Man

Now the birth of Jesus the Messiah took place in this way. When his mother Mary had been engaged to Joseph, but before they lived together, she was found to be with child from the Holy Spirit. Her husband Joseph, being a righteous man and unwilling to expose her to public disgrace, planned to dismiss her quietly. But just when he had resolved to do this, an angel of the Lord appeared to him in a dream and said, "Joseph, son of David, do not be afraid to take Mary as your wife, for the child conceived in her is from the Holy Spirit."

Matthew 1:18-25

Mary didn't know what to do. How would she break the news to Joe? They had only been dating for six weeks, but she knew that he loved her. She could see it in his eyes. And she knew that she loved him. He was so gentle and understanding. There weren't many men in the world like Joe.

Mary had met Joe in the emergency room on the very night of the assault, and they had been together every day since, as if it was meant to be. Joe was there waiting for a friend who had twisted an ankle in a softball game. She sat next to him in the waiting room before they took her in to be examined. Mary had been too upset to talk, and Joe hadn't tried to make conversation. He didn't even ask what had happened. He simply looked at her with tenderness and said, "It will be okay. They will take care of you." Even those few words had been enough to create a bond between them. And Joe had come back later, after he took his friend home, to see if she was all right. By then Mary was able to talk a little bit about the rape: the horror she had felt during the attack and the humiliation and

20

anger that were still growing within her. She was grateful for his presence. Somehow it was easier to talk about it with him than with the counselor who had been assigned to her case. Joe had listened quietly for several hours that night, and had called or come to keep her company every night since, gradually coaxing her out of her small apartment into the world again.

Joe had never once tried to touch her, and Mary loved him for that. He seemed to know without her saying it that she couldn't stand to be touched — not yet. Soon, maybe. She had found herself longing for that moment and wondering what it would be like during the past couple of weeks. Mary knew that Joe would wait until she gave him a sign, and she had thought that it might be tonight. But, when she let him know what the doctor had told her today, would Joe want to touch her? Was this the end of her hope that their love would lead to marriage and a family? What would Joe do when she told him about the baby?

Author's Note: An alternate story titled "People Of The Eyes," which is based on the psalm for this Sunday can be found in Appendix A.

In A Land Of Deep Darkness . . .

*The people who walked in darkness have seen a great
light; those who lived in a land of deep darkness —
on them light has shined.*

Isaiah 9:2

In almost any other setting Memorial's modern brick building, surrounded by neatly trimmed evergreen shrubs and an
expansive lawn, would be considered picturesque, inviting: the
kind of church you might want to visit if you happened to be
driving around on a Sunday morning, looking for a place to
worship. But surrounded, as it is on three sides, by row after
row of austere, box-shaped tenements with peeling paint and
littered sidewalks, it appears strangely out of place.

Pastor Guiseppe Basacca started the congregation as an
Italian mission in 1916, beginning with night school classes in
English, sewing and Christian doctrine. Worship services on
Sunday afternoon were begun later. In 1919 the Evangelical
General Conference made funds available, and a building was
erected at 2011 52nd Street. First Church, as it was known then,
experienced many years of persecution. Italians were subject
to severe discrimination in Kenosha at the turn of the century.
They were kept out of the good jobs and nice neighborhoods,
and generally castigated for their foreign ways, like every other
immigrant group before and after them. There were many
difficult growing pains, but the congregation endured and their
numbers increased greatly in the boom years after World War
II. They soon outgrew the old building.

Land was purchased on the edge of the city in 1956, and
the congregation built and moved into the present building at
3712 50th Street in 1960. They had high hopes. Kenosha was
expanding rapidly, and the open land all around the new

building was zoned for single-family dwellings. Their large corner lot allowed plenty of room for expansion. But a change was made in the zoning laws; the land across the street in front of the church was re-zoned for light industry. A trucking firm moved in, and its parking lot was soon packed with large car carriers loaded with new Ramblers from the American Motors plant five blocks away. The open land behind the church was re-zoned for multi-family structures. Developers began to build low-rent apartment buildings, one after another, year after year, until there were more than 90 buildings covering every available lot. No land was reserved for a park, back-yards were small and shade trees were few and far between. Children played on the sidewalks and in the streets.

The apartments filled up fast as people came from all over southern Wisconsin and northern Illinois seeking to join the 15,000-member work force at American Motors. None stayed in the apartments very long. The high wages paid by the auto manufacturer enabled them to move into homes of their own in better neighborhoods with parks and trees. Then came the next wave of new immigrants: African-Americans and Hispanics. Like the Italians before them, they, too, were kept out of the good jobs, and so they have stayed in the apartments, raising large families in crowded conditions in the neighborhood that is now called the new ghetto.

Memorial's all-white congregation, which peaked in 1971 with a membership of 195 and an average weekly worship attendance of 118, has declined to 77 members and an average worship attendance of 44. Their high hopes for a growing program and additions to their beautiful building have not been realized, in spite of the fact that their neighborhood has more people per square block than any other neighborhood in the city. The barriers of race and poverty have proved insurmountable. They have tried over the years, with little success, to reach out to families in the neighborhood. People would respond once or twice, in small numbers, to a dinner or a service, but they didn't come back. The congregation watched with an ever-deepening sense of helplessness as conditions in the neighborhood grew worse and worse.

Lately, gangs have moved in from Chicago and recruited local youths and children, some as young as eight years old, to assist in their drug deals. Break-ins, muggings, beatings and drive-by shootings are reported regularly. Gun shots are often heard in the night as gangs battle over turf. In the fall of 1990, a member of the Black Gangster Disciples was standing on the front lawn of the church when a group of Vice Lords fired at him once from a moving car. The local paper quoted him as saying he fired back at them six times, emptying his handgun.

In spite of all this, the church has not given up hope. It is determined to share its ministry with the people of the neighborhood. The building has been used for several years as a mcalsite for the county's summer lunch program. In recent months, what is called the Church For Kids program is held on Wednesdays after school. About 50 children receive a nutritious snack before going to classes, divided by age level, to study Bible lessons and sing Sunday School songs. On Tuesday and Thursday mornings the church provides a nursery for children whose parents are trying to complete their high school education at the local technical school. The church has hired an African-American organist, and some families from the neighborhood have begun attending worship on Sunday mornings. Two adults have become members.

All of this has come about because of something wonderful that happened last year at the Christmas Eve service. It began with a suggestion the pastor made at the November board meeting. "Let's invite the neighborhood kids to a Christmas party," he said. "They are used to coming here for the summer lunch program. Let's give them a party on Christmas Eve and invite them to join us at the candlelight service afterward." Everyone agreed that it was worth a try.

Posters and sign-up sheets were distributed throughout the neighborhood. Parents were asked to register their children in advance, and to come with them to the party and the service. They expected about 50 children to sign up. But when the registration sheets started coming in, it was soon apparent there were going to be many, many more. Church members donated extra money for gifts and food. The Breakfast Kiwanis Club gave a generous donation. The church women's mission group gave the pastor a blank check. "Go get the gifts," they said. "Spend whatever you need to spend."

On Christmas Eve, about 20 volunteers from the church and the neighborhood met early to wrap the gifts. When the children arrived they were met at the door and divided into small groups with an adult leader who took them around the Fellowship Hall, from one activity to another. There was a storytelling corner, a table for coloring and cutting out Christmas trees, a visit with Santa, and, of course, everyone joined in singing Christmas carols around the piano. More than 250 persons attended the party, including 133 children. About $700 worth of toys, food and candy were distributed.

The congregation decided afterward that serving the cake and punch and opening the presents just before the service may have been a mistake. The children were so excited there was no way to get them to sit still or be quiet when they went into the sanctuary. Church members who came for the traditional, peaceful candlelight service were a bit overwhelmed. Some expressed outright disapproval. "We've been trying to keep these people out of the church for years, and now they have let them all in," was one comment that was overheard.

Those who welcomed the neighborhood families felt a deep sense of satisfaction as parents shook their hands and thanked them for giving their children a Christmas party, and, most important they said, for allowing them to share in the worship service. The pastor said he got enough hugs and kisses from children with sticky, candy bar lips, to last him a lifetime.

The full meaning of what happened that night, in their little white church in the neediest African-American neighborhood in the city, sank in gradually as they cleaned up the building, put away the Christmas decorations for another year, and drove wearily to their homes for Christmas celebrations with their own families in neighborhoods far from the church. They realized that, for some of these families, this was the only Christmas they would have. And they knew, now, why God had brought them out of their old Italian neighborhood and kept them faithful all of these years in this new ghetto — to give them this extraordinary blessing. Their lives and the church they loved would never be the same again. And they knew, too, that whatever the future might bring for Memorial United Methodist Church and the neighborhood around it, for a few hours on Christmas Eve, in a land of deep darkness, a great light had shined — and they had seen it.

Author's Note: Thanks to Memorial Church members Frank Splitek, Jackie Putman, Ethel Parise, Pastor Jeff Nicholas and former pastor Merlin Hoeft, whose contributions made the telling of this story possible.

Dream Warning

. . . an angel of the Lord appeared to Joseph in a dream and said, "Get up, take the child and his mother, and flee to Egypt, and remain there until I tell you; for Herod is about to search for the child, to destroy him." Then Joseph got up, took the child and his mother by night, and went to Egypt . . .

Matthew 2:13-14

"We are going to move," the father announced one morning as the family gathered for breakfast in the kitchen of their tiny, third floor apartment. The mother gave him a bewildered look and one of the small children began to cry, but they didn't ask him for an explanation and he didn't offer one. The tone of his voice said it all. They packed as fast as they could with little conversation. By nightfall all of their belongings were loaded into a rental truck, and they were on their way to look for another apartment on the far side of the city. They stayed in a shelter that night and moved into the new apartment the next day. It was smaller and shabbier than the one they had left behind, but the best that could be found on short notice for the amount they could afford to pay.

They heard about the fire in their old apartment building on the six o'clock news. Seven of their former neighbors, including two children, had been killed. More than a dozen families were left homeless. That was when he told them about the dream. "I saw the flames," he said, "and I knew it was coming soon." That's all he would say, and none of them ever asked him about it again. But they were always grateful for the strange dream warning that had persuaded him to get them out of danger in time.

Almost In Heaven

*Then I saw a new heaven and a new earth; for the
first heaven and the first earth had passed away, and
the sea was no more. And I saw the holy city, the
new Jerusalem, coming down out of heaven from
God, prepared as a bride adorned for her husband.
And I heard a loud voice from the throne . . . .*
                                            Revelation 21:1-3a

In 1977, about 10 years before she died, I asked my grandmother, Nellie Jane Kittle Sumwalt, then in her early 80s, if
she would allow me to tape record some of her family stories.
Grandma had plenty to tell. She told me about my great, great-
grandmother, Catherine Isbell. She said that there is a town
called Isabella, Oklahoma, which was named for her. It was
supposed to have been called Isbell, but when the charter came
back from the territorial governor's office, a clerk had changed
it to Isabella — and so that is the way it has remained. But
that is another story.

Catherine Isbell and her three oldest sons claimed 640 acres
of Black Jack woods in the Oklahoma land rush of 1889: 160
acres each, as the Homestead Act allowed. They immediately
set about clearing some of the timber so they could plant crops,
and they began to build a house. It was a combination dugout,
like the sod houses they were accustomed to in Kansas, and
logs, which had been a rarity in the prairie country from which
they had come. In a few years there was a general store, which
also served as the post office, a church, and eventually a school.
Catherine was the moving force behind all of the building —
especially the church. She insisted that there be a place for the
children to attend worship and Sunday school.

Catherine never missed an opportunity to witness to her
faith: to tell how God had blessed her throughout her life. All

of her extra money was sent to missions. When Catherine visited her grandchildren, she always held what she called "family worship." She would gather everyone around her and tell stories from the Bible, and then, as Grandma tells it, "We would all join in singing the old gospel hymns that were her favorites." Grandma said, "My folks were not much for going to church but when Grandma Catherine came, she took my oldest brother Elmer and I to church every Sunday. Pa let us drive the horse and the spring wagon to church by ourselves after Grandma Catherine had gone home. One Sunday the wagon got stuck in the mud as we were crossing the creek. That was the end of going to church for a while, but Elmer and I never forgot what we had learned."

There were not many doctors in that part of the country in those days, so Catherine became the community midwife. She helped to deliver over 100 babies in her time. She always prayed during the deliveries and the Lord always answered her prayers. Catherine was very proud of the fact that she never lost a mother or a baby.

My great, great-grandmother Catherine died of pneumonia at the age of 83. The way Grandma tells it, she was out making garden on a cold day when she shouldn't have been. It had rained the night before, and she crawled around on the damp ground and took sick. She was unconscious by the time her daughter Liza and grandson Elmer arrived from Texhoma. They called the doctor, and when he arrived he gave her a shot, which revived her. When she came to, she was angry. She raised her head up, looked around at everyone and said, "Ohhh, I was almost in heaven! I could see across the river; I could see over there and it was beautiful. And then the devil came along and poked his spear in my arm, and here I am back in the world!"

When Grandma had finished telling this and several other stories, I knew something about myself that I hadn't known before. I knew where my faith came from. From my great, great-grandmother, handed down through my grandmother to me.

Granna

. . . "He who scattered Israel will gather him and will keep him as a shepherd a flock." For the Lord has ransomed Jacob, and has redeemed him from hands too strong for him. They shall come and sing aloud on the height of Zion, and they shall be radiant over the goodness of the Lord, over the grain, the wine, the oil . . .

Jeremiah 31:10b-12a

"I was born in a refugee camp, near the end of the last great war. We lived there until I was almost eight years old. I remember because we got word that we were going home on the eve of my eighth birthday. Oh, what a time it was."

The teenage boy smiled and moved his chair closer to the old woman's bed. He had heard the story a hundred times before, but he was glad to hear it again: glad that his grandmother was able to say anything at all. Sometimes she went for days at a time without saying a word, not recognizing anyone on the nursing home staff, or any of the several family members who came often to see her. But the sound of her grandson's voice always seemed to bring her back. She would touch his face and say, "Jimmy, it's you." And then they would talk, as they always had since he was a small boy.

"Tell me about Granna," he said. It was his favorite part of the long saga of her life in the refugee camp. And so the old woman would tell the tale again.

"We were always hungry," she said. "Sometimes the fighting was so fierce around the camp that several weeks would pass before the relief trucks came with our rations. Father and Mother would make what food we had last as long as they could, eating very little themselves so that we children would

30

have enough to keep us alive. There were many occasions when we were so weak from hunger that we had no strength to chase each other on the muddy paths between the tents, as we did when our bellies were full. It was then that she would gather all of us around her up on the hill, on the dry rocks overlooking the camp. 'It is story time,' she would say as she began to hobble up the path, pulling herself along with a cut off section of metal pipe that she used as a cane. The word spread fast, and soon there would be more than 100 hungry children gathered around her on the rocks. There was always at least one little one on her lap, cuddled in close to the old, frayed army blanket that she wore over her shoulders like a shawl. Her name was Rachel, but she was known throughout the camp as Granna. It was the name one of the little ones had given to her — his way of saying grandma. And so, that's what we called her, for she was grandmother to us all.

"She always began by telling us how our people were once slaves in Egypt, how their cruel captors forced them to make bricks in the hot sun, and how God sent Moses to set them free and lead them through the wilderness to the promised land. She told of the day God sent quails into their camp when they were hungry, and after that gave them manna to gather from the ground each morning. She made the story sound so real, and we were so hungry, that we could almost taste the tender meat of the roasted birds and the sweet bread baked from the manna. We used to look for manna on the ground around our tents, but we never found anything that was edible. The sand and pebbles that we did gather were mixed into a mud cake batter and baked on hot rocks by the fire. When the cakes were done, we covered them with imaginary honey and jam and pretended to eat them.

"Our favorite story of all those Granna told us from the 'Big Book,' as she called it, was the tale of Elijah, the Tishbite and the Ravens. 'Elijah was a mighty prophet,' she would say, and then in a deep, dramatic voice she would recount the words he spoke to the wicked king who was oppressing his people. 'As the Lord God of Israel lives, before whom I stand, there shall be neither dew nor rain these years, except by my word.' And then, she said, the rain stopped and there was no longer any morning dew. The King became so angry with Elijah that he had to flee for his life. God told him to go and hide beside a small stream in the desert. So the prophet went and lived by the stream, and great black birds called ravens brought him bread and meat twice a day, in the morning and in the evening.

"When the hunger pains in our swollen stomachs were the worst, we used to scan the skies looking for ravens. Who knew, maybe God would send us bread and meat, too.

"And then on one of those awful, hungry days that I shall never forget, we heard the sound of engines overhead and felt the force of a great wind on our faces. There were three large cargo helicopters hovering over the camp. Soon we saw parachutes open above our heads and begin to float gently to the earth carrying big cartons of food and supplies. We ran to the spot where they fell, hundreds of us, pushing and shoving, grabbing for anything we could find to eat. Lucky for us, one of the first boxes that broke open contained fresh apples. We gobbled down the apples and we danced and sang around the camp in anticipation of the feast that we knew was to come as soon as the rations had been divided.

"After we had eaten, Granna gathered us all together again on the rocks above the camp, and this time, instead of telling us a story, she taught us how to say thanks to the One who had sent us food to eat.

"Granna's stories saved our lives," the old woman sighed, "Oh, what a time it was."

One day when the boy came to the nursing home to see her, the old woman would not respond. He sat with her quietly for a while, holding onto one of her tired hands. And then he tried again. "Granna," he said, "are you there?" Slowly there appeared in her eyes a glimmer of recognition. "Jimmy," she said, "It's you."

Author's Note: This story is dedicated to my favorite mother-in-law, Phyllis Hunter Perry, who is known to her grandchildren as Granna.

Between A Rock And A Hard Place

---

*I waited patiently for the Lord; he inclined to me
and heard my cry. He drew me up from the deso-
late pit, out of the miry bog, and set my feet upon
a rock, making my steps secure.*

Psalm 40:1-2b

There is a high hill which overlooks the little city of Richland Center, in south west Wisconsin where I grew up. I'll never
forget the night I climbed that hill and literally ended up between a rock and a hard place. About three-fourths of the way
up the hill, where the path makes a wide bend on a natural
plateau, there is a large opening in the trees which allows an
unobstructed view of the city below. The rock, a slab of sand-
stone nearly four feet high and seven or eight inches wide, lay
at a 45-degree angle, about 20 feet off the path. It was leaning against a pile of smaller rocks, and it appeared to me that
all that was needed was a little pull and it would be level enough
to sit upon: the perfect perch from which to contemplate the
view and smoke one of the cheap cigars I was carrying in my
pocket. I tugged at it and quickly discovered that it was much
heavier than it appeared. I pulled again, with all of my might,
and it came forward, on top of me, pinning both of my legs
fast to the ground. With much effort I was able to raise it a
few inches off my mid-section, but I was not able to lift it high
enough to free either of my legs.

After several minutes of futile pushing and straining, I became resigned to the fact that I would never be able to free
myself from the rock. I began to pray and to wonder as I
prayed how long it might be before someone wandered up the
hill and discovered me in my predicament. I knew that work-
men came up periodically to do maintenance on the telephone

33

and radio towers on the peak, but I didn't know how often, and I began to doubt that I could survive there, exposed to the elements as I was, for more than three or four days.

It was then that I heard myself yelling for help at the top of my voice. The cry came as a reflex. I made no conscious decision to call out. I was so far above the city that, had I reflected the wisdom of sounding a distress call, I probably would have decided that it was useless and saved my breath.

The police arrived about 10 minutes after I began to call for help. The two of them were able to lift the rock easily from my legs. They laughed at me as I tried to explain how and why I had managed to pull the rock on top of myself. I suffered this small humiliation happily and thanked them again and again for saving my life as they loaded me into the ambulance. Sometime after I was released from the hospital, with no apparent damage done to anything but my pride, I learned that it was an aquaintance of my family, an old preacher's widow who lived in a small house just over the brow of the hill, who heard my cry for help and called the police.

I now live far away from Richland Center, and I have long since given up cigars, but I have never forgotten what happened that night, and I never cease to give thanks to the one who heard my cry and delivered me from that rock and hard place.

Author's Note: This story is dedicated in loving memory of Mrs. Lester Matthews, the one whose neighborliness was the answer to my prayer for deliverance.

Steve's Call

*As he walked by the Sea of Galilee, he saw two
brothers, Simon, who is called Peter, and Andrew
his brother, casting a net into the sea — for they
were fishermen. And he said to them, "Follow me,
and I will make you fish for people." Immediately
they left their nets and followed him.*

Matthew 4:18-20

It all started with two questions put to me by my grandmother during one of our family's regular Sunday afternoon
visits with her in the nursing home where she spent the last
three years of her life. She was always glad to see us. There
were smiles and hugs all around every Sunday. But once in
a while she would let her guard down and tell us just how
difficult life had become for her. Grandma had outlived her
husband and two of her sons, and she was bedridden. One
day she said to me, "Why doesn't God let me die?" That was
the first question. Naively, I said what many of us have said
in response to questions like that; "Maybe God has something
more for you to do." These words would prove to be prophetic.
Years later I would recognize that moment as the beginning
of what was to be a great change in my life.

The second question was much less dramatic than the first.
Grandma simply asked, "What did the preacher say in church
today?" We had to admit that we didn't know, because we
hadn't been in church that day. We knew that we didn't dare
tell her any stories, because the pastor called on her regularly
and she was sure to find out the truth. We went to worship
the following Sunday, and every Sunday after that, so that
we could give Grandma accurate reports about the content of
the services. Sometimes we actually took notes during the
sermon so that we wouldn't forget what the preacher said.

This went on for about a year, and as the Sundays passed we found ourselves more and more drawn to the gospel message. One day, my wife and I both realized that we were going to worship for ourselves, because we wanted to go, and not just so we could give a good report to Grandma. We became excited about God and the church. It was a genuine conversion experience for both of us. Christ became real to us for the first time in our lives. Grandma didn't have to pump us to tell her about church anymore. We shared without being asked, because we couldn't help ourselves.

That's how it all started, but that was only the beginning. God wasn't finished with me yet. A few months later, at the end of the ordination service at Annual Conference, the Bishop invited everyone who felt called into ordained ministry to come forward to the altar. I had a very strong feeling that I ought to go. It felt like someone was tugging at me, urging me to go. I didn't understand what was happening to me. My father and I had just purchased a business together. It was no time to be thinking of a career change, so I overruled the feeling. I remember literally hanging onto my chair to prevent myself from going forward.

But that wasn't the end of it, either. In the next few years the Spirit led me into a deeper and deeper relationship with God. I became a certified lay speaker in the church, and I continued to feel strong urgings to enter the ordained ministry. In the summer of 1982, our pastor said to me one day, "Steve, when are you going to go to seminary?" I had a sinking feeling in my stomach. I knew he was right, but I didn't want to admit it. I began to wrestle with God every day and every night. I couldn't concentrate on my work and I wasn't sleeping well. I had this recurring vision where I saw myself in seminary. Finally, in desperation, I prayed to God, "If you really want me in ministry, I'm willing, but you will have to open some doors for me." I didn't know it at the time, but the doors had already been opened. Grandma's questions had pointed the way, and I'm sure now that her prayers opened the doors.

36

By December of that same year I was enrolled as a fresh-man at the university. It would take me seven long years to complete my college and seminary education. But I had no doubts after I made up my mind to say yes to God's call. For the first time in years I was at peace with myself and God.

Author's Note: The Reverend Stephen Groves graduated from The University of Dubuque Theological Seminary in June of 1990. He serves as pastor of the Loyal-York Center Charge in the Wisconsin Conference of the United Methodist Church. Steve's grandmother, Mayme Marks, died in August of 1977 after her work here on earth was finished. It was five years later that the seed she planted in Steve took root and grew.

Mercy, Mercy

Blessed are the merciful, for they shall receive mercy.
Matthew 5:7

There was once a little girl named Mercy. Isn't that an unusual name? Mercy didn't think it was unusual, because it had always been her name and seemed perfectly normal to her. In fact, her mom had told her that it is a very special name, which means to show kindness to someone in need or to forgive someone who has wronged you, even though they don't deserve to be forgiven.

One day, Mercy and some of her friends were playing tag in the backyard when a baby robin fell from somewhere overhead and hit the ground with a loud plop in front of them. When they looked up, they could see that it had fallen out of a nest in a large oak tree which stood on the edge of Mercy's yard. One of the children picked up the dazed bird and threw it into the air to see if it could fly. But the poor bird was too young to fly, and it hit the ground again with a thud. "Oh, be careful," Mercy said. "We mustn't hurt it. We must put it back in the nest so its mother can take care of it until it learns to fly."

Very gently, so as not to harm it, Mercy picked up the little bird. She tucked it into the soft corner of her pocket, carefully climbed up into the oak tree, and placed it back into the nest with its brothers and sisters. The little bird seemed glad to be home.

Mercy felt very good about what she had done. But as she was thinking about how proud her mother would be when she told her about it, something terrible happened. She slipped as she was climbing down and fell out of the tree, right on top of one of her neighbor's prize-winning rose bushes. She didn't

38

fall far, so she wasn't badly hurt: just a scratch and a couple of bruises. But the rose bush was smashed, and Mercy knew it was her neighbor's favorite.

When Mercy looked up, her neighbor, Mrs. Black, was standing over her, looking down at the broken rose bush. She had been watching from the window. Mercy was scared. She was certain that Mrs. Black was going to yell at her, and worse yet, probably tell her mother. Then she wouldn't be allowed to play with her friends for a week.

Mrs. Black helped Mercy up off the rose bush. It was broken near the base, and there was no hope at all that it could be saved. Mercy waited for the worst. Mrs. Black said, "Mercy, I saw what you did. It was very good of you to help that poor little bird. It was a kind and merciful thing to do. It's too bad about the rose bush. I know you didn't mean to break it, so I'm not going to say anything to your mother. But, the next time you need to climb a tree, please remember to ask a grown-up to help you."

Mercy was very happy that she wasn't going to be punished. And she never forgot, for as long as she lived, how Mrs. Black had shown her mercy.

The Well-worn Path

Happy are those whose way is blameless, who walk in the law of the Lord. Happy are those who keep his decrees, who seek him with their whole heart, who also do no wrong, but walk in his ways.

Psalm 119:1-3

He has told you, O Mortal, what is good; and what does the Lord require of you but to do justice, and to love kindness, and to walk humbly with your God?

Micah 6:8 (Epiphany 4)

Old Pilgrim Community Church, as it was known to long-time residents of the city, stood like a fortress in the middle of the mostly abandoned downtown business district. The auditorium was still there, along with the post office, the courthouse and the library, but must of the stores and business offices had long since been moved to nicer settings in the suburbs. The old church, which had always been a great source of pride to its members, remained a monument to the inner city's once glorious past. Most members of the congregation drove 20 or 30 minutes to attend services on Sunday mornings. No programs and few meetings were held there during the week, because the neighborhood around the church wasn't safe after dark. The main focus of the congregation's ministry was the upkeep of their building. There was always plenty of money to keep it in mint condition.

It was about three years after they put in the new carpeting that they first noticed the path that ran all the way around the perimeter of the sanctuary. It appeared in patches at first: what they would have assumed were normal wear marks if it

40

were not for the fact that they occurred in low as well as high traffic areas of the carpeting. There was one curved wear mark that extended all the way from the end of the front row pew, past the baptismal font, almost to the center aisle. A similar mark could be seen curving past the paino bench on the other side of the sanctuary. There were also wear marks which circled the ends of the back pews, but these at least made some sense, because nearly half of the congregation walked around one or the other on their way to and from the side aisles every Sunday morning. It was when all of the wear marks became connected into one distinct path, encircling the entire worship area, that they knew they were confronted with a peculiar mystery. Who or what was making the path?

The chairperson of the church board called a special meeting to discuss the path. No one seemed to know what was causing it. Some theorized that it might be the kids tearing around in the sanctuary after the youth fellowship meetings, but a call to the youth adviser persuaded them otherwise. There were some jokes about the church ghost leaving a visible trail, but no logical explanations were offered by any of the board members. The meeting was adjourned after a motion to replace the carpeting was tabled until it could be determined what was causing the path. The chairperson encouraged them to keep their eyes open and report back at the next meeting.

Two years passed. The path was now worn even deeper into the carpeting, and nearly everyone in the congregation was aware of the enigma concerning its origin. It was the subject of much light-hearted discussion during the coffee hours after worship and at most of the church's regular committee meetings. The pastor brought it up in sermons from time to time. There was an article about the path in the local newspaper. Visitors stopped in just to see for themselves and to offer their own explanations. Many returned and became members of the church. The strange conundrum of the carpet path added to the already considerable prestige enjoyed by the congregation. Some still wanted to replace the carpet, but most agreed that the path was an asset, so the replacement plan was postponed indefinitely. The congregation was quite content to live with their rewarding and comfortable mystery.

Then one cold January night, when the temperature dipped to 30 below zero, the custodian drove in from the suburbs to check on the boiler. Just as he was about to leave the building he noticed some movement in the sanctuary. His first thought was to call the police. No one had any business being in the church at such a late hour. But as he peered through the narthex window, he thought he recognized the person he saw moving slowly about among the shadows. He opened the door, stepped quietly into the sanctuary, and watched for a few minutes until his eyes had adjusted to the darkness. Sure enough, it was old Roy Lincoln, the retired shoemaker whose little shop, with its upstairs apartment, had stood across the street from the church. He hadn't been around in years. Someone said he had moved to the hotel on the other side of the courthouse. He watched as Roy walked slowly, following the path full circle around the pews. He appeared to be talking to himself as he walked.

"Is that you, Roy?" the custodian called out in a loud voice. "What are you doing up so late on a cold night?"

"Oh, hi Sid," Roy said. "I didn't hear you come in. I'm just walking and praying. I can't kneel anymore, and I need the exercise, so I just pray while I walk. Sometimes I talk to God, and sometimes I listen while God talks to me. I pray for the lonely and the sick: for the families I know are grieving, and for my friends on the street. You don't mind that I'm here, do you Sid? This has always been my church."

"No," Sid said, "I don't mind. Just be sure the door is locked when you leave."

The next morning, when Sid saw the pastor, he told him that the mystery of the carpet path had been solved. Then he told him all about Sid's walking and praying.

Word spread fast through the congregation that Roy Lincoln was the cause of the path in the sanctuary carpet. There was no more talk of replacing the carpet after that. When visitors came, the members would point to the path with pride and tell about Roy's walking and praying. Sometimes some of them would stop at the church late at night and walk with him as he prayed.

It was on one of these occasions that someone offered to give Roy a ride home.

"I am home," Roy said. "This is where I sleep. I thought everybody knew that. Since I lost my room a few years ago, I've been sleeping up in the balcony storage room. I haven't had anywhere else to go."

When the church board met the following night they had a new problem to consider, and it wasn't a comfortable mystery.

"Perhaps we could open a shelter for the homeless in some of our spare rooms." It was one of the newer members who spoke. "Then Roy and the other street people in our neighborhood would have a warm place to sleep."

His suggestion was followed by a long, uncomfortable silence. Everyone knew that it was the right thing to do, but no one wanted to be responsible for doing it.

"Maybe we need to pray about it," the pastor said. "I suggest we go into the sanctuary and pray for a while." One by one, the board members followed behind him as he led the way to the well-worn path.

The Master Builder

According to the grace of God given to me, like a skilled master builder I laid a foundation, and someone else is building on it. Each builder must choose with care how to build on it. For no one can lay any foundation other than the one that has been laid; that foundation is Jesus Christ.

1 Corinthians 3:10-11

There were once two young men who wanted to be carpenters. In order to learn the craft, they both apprenticed themselves to a master carpenter. They served as his assistants for a number of years, at first fetching and carrying, pounding and sawing, and gradually taking on the more difficult tasks, until at last they could to everything the master could do.

One day after work, the master called them aside and said, "I've taught you everything I know. You have mastered all of the basic skills of carpentry. The only thing you lack is experience. It is time for each of you to go into business for yourself, but before you go I want to give you some final words of advice. Be honest in all of your dealings. Always do your best work, even if it means doing a job over again and taking a loss. Practice safety first, as I have taught you. Buy good, quality tools and take proper care of them so that they will last. And, most importantly, share all that you know generously with those who come to learn from you. If you do all of these things you will become known for your good work, and you will prosper."

Both men remembered well what the master had taught them. They were honest in all of their dealings. They always did their best, even if it meant losing money. They maintained good safety practices. They bought the best tools that were available, and they took good care of them. They became known far and wide for their good work. Neither of them ever lacked for projects, and many apprentices came to learn from them.

The first carpenter taught his apprentices as he had been taught, simple tasks first. He gradually allowed them to do the things that required more skill, until at last they were able to use the big power tools, as he did. Apprentices flocked to him, his business expanded more each year, and he became quite a wealthy man.

The second carpenter allowed his apprentices to do simple tasks, but would never let them operate his big power tools. They cost too much money, he said. It would be better if he operated them himself. Then he could be sure that they were properly maintained and that they would last a long time.

His apprentices always left in frustration after a few months. Soon no apprentices came to him to learn the trade. His business declined, and after a time he was unable to pay his bills. The bank had to foreclose on his mortgage. They took his truck, his power tools, and all of the rest of his equipment, and sold them at public auction.

Knowing And Doing Right

*Teach me, O Lord, the way of your statutes, and
I will observe it to the end. Give me understanding,
that I may keep your law and observe it with my
whole heart. Lead me in the path of your command-
ments, for I delight in it . . . See, I have longed for
your precepts; in your righteousness give me life.*
                                        Psalm 119:33-35, 40

There was once a little boy named Jimmy who always
wanted to know what was right and what was wrong in every
situation. He continually pestered his parents with questions
about right and wrong. No matter who he was with or where
they were, sooner or later he would ask a question about right
and wrong.

"Dad," he would say, "I saw some kids eating grapes in
the grocery store, and they didn't pay for them when they left.
They said they only took a few and were sure no one would
miss them. Is that right?"

"No, it's not right," his Dad said. "You should never take
anything from a store without paying for it, even something
as small as a grape. What those kids did was stealing. The store
owners have to pay for everything they have for sale. When
people steal things the stores have to raise prices on other items
to make up the difference. People who take things without
paying are really stealing from everyone who shops in the store.
It's just not right."

"I'll try to remember that," said Jimmy.

Or, Jimmy would say, "Mom, is it ever all right to break
a rule?" "Well," his mom said, pausing to think about the
question, "there might be some very rare instances when the
only loving thing to do would be to break a rule. But those

kinds of situations are very rare. I don't think you need to worry about it."

"I'll have to think about that," Jimmy said. He tried to imagine a situation where breaking a rule would be the loving thing to do, but he couldn't think of a single instance where he would be willing to break a rule. He had almost forgotten about the question when something drastic happened that forced him to make a life or death decision that involved breaking a rule.

It happened one day when Jimmy and his grandpa were fishing in a motor boat out on the lake. It was a beautiful day, and they were having a wonderful time telling stories and drinking pop as they fished. Jimmy's grandpa was a great storyteller, and Jimmy loved to listen to him tell about all the big fish he had caught. He didn't mind that the fish seemed to get bigger each time Grandpa told about them. Suddenly, in the middle of one of Jimmy's favorite fish stories, his grandpa clutched his chest and fell forward into the middle of the boat. He lay there without moving or saying a word. Jimmy tried to turn him over, but he was too heavy. He could tell that Grandpa was breathing, but he knew he was very sick and needed to see a doctor as soon as possible.

Jimmy was scared. He had never been more scared in all of his life. There they were, in a boat out in the middle of the lake. His grandpa had told him never to start the motor or to try to operate the boat by himself. Grandpa said, "When you are old enough, I'll teach you how to drive the boat." Jimmy didn't know what to do. He tried rowing the boat, but he wasn't strong enough to work the oars. He felt like crying, but he knew that wouldn't do any good. He knew that he had to do something and do it soon, because if he didn't his grandpa might die.

He prayed, "Dear God, what is the right thing to do?" And then he knew. He would have to start the motor and try to drive the boat. It was the only way to save his grandpa's life.

The motor started with one pull. Now came the hard part. Jimmy had never driven anything but a bicycle. But he had watched his grandpa drive the boat many times. He did what he remembered seeing Grandpa do, and they were off. The boat didn't go perfectly straight, but he managed to get it back to the shore. Then he ran to the nearest house and called for help. An ambulance came and took his grandpa to the hospital. The doctor told him later that they got him there just in the nick of time. A few more minutes, and they would not have been able to save him.

When Jimmy went into the hospital room to see his grandpa, he was a little bit afraid of what Grandpa might say about him driving the boat, but he needn't have worried. When his grandpa saw him, he smiled and gave him a big hug. And then he said, "Jimmy, you did just the right thing. Your quick thinking saved my life."

Jimmy smiled back at his grandpa. His heart was full of joy. He was glad he had done the right thing. Soon he was back in the employ of the master carpenter seeking to learn again the secret of successful building.

Author's Note: This story was told as part of a consecration day sermon at Trinity United Methodist Church in Montello, Wisconsin, June 9, 1985. It is shared here in honor of the building committee: Eleanor Steinhaus, Herb Sheller, Linda Tanner, Wayne Reiche, Shelley Robinson, Krista Sherin, Jim Paul, Fred Cartwright, chairperson Bill Dow, architect Dick Thern, master builder Sherman Schneider and June Norton who helped to plan the kitchen just before she died.

Cleansed

Have mercy on me, O God, according to your stead-fast love; according to your abundant mercy blot out my transgressions. Wash me thoroughly from my iniquity, and cleanse me from my sin.

Psalm 51:1-2

Shirley sits bolt upright in her bed and cries out, "Enough, I can't bear it anymore!" The back of her nightgown is soaked with perspiration and she is trembling. It is the same nightmare, night after night. She sees herself going out the door of the discount store with toys and clothes for her children hidden carefully in the lining of her coat. A large man wearing a blue blazer and a red tie approaches and politely asks her to show him a receipt for the merchandise under her coat. She begins to run. The man grabs her arm, pushes her up against a wall and handcuffs her to a shopping cart. She sees other customers staring at her as they go in and out of the store. She knows that they know what she has been doing. It is at this point that she always wakes up with a feeling of excruciating, unredeemable guilt.

Shirley can no longer live with the guilt. She gets up, changes into a dry nightgown, sits down at the desk, and writes: "Dear Sir, I have been shoplifting merchandise from your store regularly for the past five years. I do not know the exact value of all the items I have stolen, but I am certain that the total exceeds $1,000. I am deeply sorry for what I have done, and I promise you I will never do it again. I am prepared to repay what I have taken with interest if you will allow me to make monthly payments over a period of two years."

Before there is time to change her mind Shirley signs the note and seals it in an envelope addressed to the manager of

49

the store. Then she puts on a robe, walks to the post office, drops it in a mail slot, and goes home to wait. On the morning of the third day after her late night posting the phone rings as she is stepping out of the shower. She wraps herself in a towel, drips down the hallway, and picks up the extension in the bedroom. It is the store manager. He tells her that they have received her note and are prepared to make a settlement. They want her to pay half of what she owes immediately, with a credit card or bank loan, and the rest in monthly payments over one year. They also insist that she see a psychologist recommended by the store. If she agrees to their terms, they will refrain from pressing charges. Shirley readily agrees and they make arrangements for her to come in and sign the necessary papers.

The following Sunday, in worship, Shirley listens as the choir sings an arrangement of Amazing Grace.

When the song is finished Shirley kneels at the communion rail with the rest of the congregation and receives the body and blood of Christ. Tears of joy run down her cheeks as she tastes the sweet bread and wine. She is cleansed.

Don't Blame The Snake

They heard the sound of the Lord God walking in the garden at the time of the evening breeze, and the man and his wife hid themselves from the presence of the Lord God among the trees of the garden. But the Lord God called to the man, and said to him, "Where are you?" He said, "I heard the sound of you in the garden, and I was afraid because I was naked; and I hid myself." He said, "Who told you that you were naked? Have you eaten from the tree of which I commanded you not to eat?" The man said, "The woman whom you gave to be with me, she gave me fruit from the tree, and I ate." Then the Lord God said to the woman, "What is this that you have done?" The woman said, "The serpent tricked me, and I ate." The Lord God said to the serpent, "Because you have done this, cursed are you among all animals and among all wild creatures; upon your belly you shall go, and dust you shall eat all the days of your life."

Genesis 3:8-14

Once upon a time there was a little boy named Herman who had a pet snake named Thurman. Now, Thurman was a silly, mischievous snake who was continually getting into one kind of trouble or another. Whenever there was spilled milk, a bite out of a birthday cake, or a hole in the screen door, it was a good bet that Thurman had had something to do with it. Herman knew this, so it wasn't long before he was blaming all of his own misdeeds on Thurman. When he broke a plate washing dishes, or tracked mud all over the kitchen floor, Thurman got the blame. He even blamed Thurman for scratching up his new bicycle.

51

One day, Herman spilled pink paint in the middle of the living room carpet. When his parents came home, you guessed it, he placed all of the blame on Thurman. His mom and dad were both very angry with Thurman. His dad said, "That's it, Thurman just has to go. He has been causing too much trouble. We will take him down to the old quarry and throw him into the snake pit. That's where naughty snakes belong."

Well, poor Herman was beside himself. He didn't know what to do. He loved Thurman very much, and he didn't want him to be thrown into the snake pit.

(What would you have done if you were Herman?)

That is just what Herman did. He hold his mom and dad the truth about all the things he had blamed on Thurman that were really his fault. But it was too late. His mom and dad didn't believe him.

The next day, they took Thurman and threw him into the snake pit with all of the other snakes. Herman was very sad and angry with himself for what he had done to Thurman. And he never forgot it for as long as he lived. Through it all, he learned a valuable lesson. He never ever again blamed someone else for something he had done.

Author's Note: I usually invite the children to bring their stuffed toy snakes to worship on the day that I tell this story. I tell the story during the children's moment and follow it with an adult sermon on sin and responsibility.

One More Time

Now the Lord said to Abram, "Go from your country and your kindred and your father's house to the land that I will show you . . ." So Abram went, as the Lord had told him . . .

Genesis 12:1, 4a

The bright sun on the leaves and the breeze stirring the tree tops outside the unshaded picture window were inviting. It was a perfect morning to go out and explore the neighborhood. But nine packing boxes, in combination with the pieces of furniture pushed here and there, left only little walkways through the living room. First things first.

The massive upright piano was the first thing to consider. Once in place it wouldn't be moved again. The movers had put it in the north corner, next to the picture window, but nothing fit around it there. On the west wall it was right next to the fire place, and the south wall was about six inches too short for it; damn whoever enlarged the doorway to the dining room! So, the east wall it would have to be, for good. The south wall was the only place where the television could be seen from all of the rest of the room, anyway, and there was something comfortable about placing the sofa next to the fireplace.

Funny, every time it came down to only one logical arrangement for the furniture, no matter what the size or shape of the living room. The recliner and the rose colored wing-back chair would fit the north side of the room, in front of the picture window, with a lamp between them on an end table. Then the pole lamp, placed to the right of the sofa, would also light the recliner. There was even room in the corner behind them for the spinning wheel. The furniture had fit, one more time, but the boxes still waited. More hands would certainly be helpful.

If only the phone would ring. If only someone would suggest taking a walk or having coffee. The sunlight was still playing with the shadows in the trees, and the breeze still blew. It was probably blowing through the trees in the yard at home, too.

Author's Note: This story was written by Jo Perry-Sumwalt.

Close Call

The snares of death encompassed me; the pangs of Sheol laid hold on me; I suffered distress and anguish. Then I called on the name of the Lord: "O Lord, I pray, save my life!"

Psalm 116:3-4

It was silo filling time, late September, in southwest Wisconsin, before the frost turned the corn brown. Leonard took the cornbinder out early on a Monday morning, after the kids left for school, and cut 10 rounds on a six-acre field they referred to as the "new ground." He and his sons had converted it from pasture to cropland the year before by hauling off several stoneboat loads of rocks and trimming back the brush and a few small trees. It gave him a good deal of satisfaction to see the fine crop of corn the field had produced in its first year. The slope on the south end of the field was a bit steep, but would be all right if they were careful on the turns.

He went back with the tractor and wagon after lunch to pick up a load of corn bundles. When the wagon was full he came down across the slope on the south end, and just as he made the turn, the wagon pushed the tractor sideways and tipped it over.

Leonard said later, "I fell off under it, and all I could see was the thing coming down on top of me. The tractor was going to be on me. The first thing I thought of was how long it would be before anybody found me — and then I blacked out, how long I don't remember, but when I came to the tractor was on top of me. My legs were sticking out beside the motor, and all four wheels of the tractor were sticking straight in the air. I was laying between the fender and the body of the tractor, and the fender was laying on my left wrist. There

I was, pinned. I could feel oil running out of the motor onto my legs. It was warm. I didn't know how I was going to get out. I laid there for a while, and then I hollered. My old dog Rover was with me, and every time I hollered, he howled. Someone went by on the ridge road, up above, but they didn't see us, so I didn't know what to do. Finally, I said to myself, 'I've got to get that tractor off my wrist somehow. ' Then I happened to think about the jackknife I always carried in my pocket. Luckily it was on my right-hand side. I got it out and started digging, thinking maybe I could dig the dirt out from under my wrist enough to free it. I dug and dug, 'til finally I had dug a hole deep enough that my hand dropped down so I could pull it out. The circulation had been cut off for some time and it was quite swollen. I pulled myself out from under the tractor, called for Rover to come, and we headed for the house.

"We got about half way home, and here come a deer up to the hill, tongue hanging out, looking like he was going to drop at any moment. I looked across the valley, and there were a couple of dogs coming. They'd been chasing the deer. Rover sat down beside me and waited. I said, 'You watch them.' The deer went on, and when the dogs got close I said, 'Rover, go get 'em.' And boy, he put the run on those dogs. They went back to where they came from. When he came back we went on down to the house, and when we got to the yard I collapsed. I hollered for Bernice and she came out and helped me get up onto the porch. She sent one of the kids down the road to the neighbor's and they came and took me to the hospital. There were no broken bones, so I was only there about a week. The following Saturday the boys from the church all came in and finished filling my silo. I got out of the hospital in time to come home and see them do it.

"That was a close call. It wasn't my time to go yet. The good Lord knew that I had a family to raise and take care of, I guess, and that was why I lived."

Author's Note: My father, A. Leonard Sumwalt, tells this story of a tractor accident that occurred on our farm in Richland County, Wisconsin, in the early 1960s. It is printed here mostly in his own words.

Last Words

*Be gracious to me, O Lord, for I am in distress; my
eye wastes away from grief, my soul and body also.
For my life is spent with sorrow, and my years with
sighing; my strength fails because of my misery, and
my bones waste away . . . My times are in your hand;
deliver me from the hand of my enemies and perse-
cutors. Let your face shine upon your servant; save
me in your steadfast love.*

                                    Psalm 31:9-10, 15-16

The family entered the funeral home with that hesitation
of dread that always accompanies funeral goers. They hung
their coats and filed dutifully into the viewing room, edging
cautiously toward the casket. Then, when their reluctant eyes
fell on the familiar gnarled hands, the soft, white hair, and
the sweet, peaceful smile on the face of their sister, mother,
aunt, grandmother, Ellen Greene, an almost audible, surprised,
pleased "Oh" formed on their lips. And when they had said
their goodbyes, they filed away into the other rooms to greet
those whose company they shared only at solemn rites, making way for the next hesitant group, for they were a large
family.

"She looks so good! How did they make her look so
natural?" everyone said, and they drifted off into more comfortable conversation. But her daughter, Mary, returned again
and again to the coffin, captivated by the sweet look that no
mortician's hand could have fashioned. Perhaps it was because
she had been so close to her mother during the last, lonely,
difficult years, that she needed to understand the smile. Looking at the softly curved old lips made her try to imagine its
source.

After Ellen was widowed, some part of her family would come nearly every weekend, all year 'round: her six sons and daughters, their spouses and children, and her great-grandchildren. Her house rang with conversation and laughter, and little ones ran, toddled and crept underfoot. Ellen sat in her rocker joyously engaged in hearing first one family's stories and then another's. There was rarely a weekend when no one came.

"I don't know why I'm still here," she often said. "I'm not any good for anything now, but I just can't seem to die."

"Oh, Grandma, don't talk that way. We all love you and need you here," they always said, and so she kept the noise and the laughter in her head during the week to share with Leon and the pictures.

Ellen's tiny living room was lined with bookshelves filled with school, graduation, wedding and baby photos. After Leon died she had used them for company. As her health failed, and her eyesight dimmed, and her life was gradually confined to her house, she found herself telling Leon about her conversations with their grandchildren and the many marriages and births he had missed.

"They're all growing up so fast," she told him in her soft, quavering voice, holding the baby pictures close enough to her wrinkled face to distinguish their tiny, blurred features. She would laugh at their antics, captured for all time, self-consciously covering her mouth, even when alone, to hide her few discolored, snaggly teeth. "They are so boo-ful. See Leon, how blessed we are."

Her life fell into a routine, each event heralded by the striking of the old Regulator clock on the wall by the porch door. She didn't rise before six o'clock, even if she had been awake to hear the striking of four and five. At seven she boiled an egg and made tea. From eight until eleven she listened to the radio and read the mail, then switched on the television for a few game shows while she ate a sandwich. Between 12:30 and 1:30 p.m. her oldest daughter, Mary, would call while she was at home for lunch and ask how Ellen was, what groceries she could bring, which bills needed to be paid, or what errands run. All afternoon Ellen would crochet or work word puzzles, and watch the traffic move by outside her window.

In time it seemed that her abilities passed more quickly than the days. Her sight was limited to blurred patches of light and darkness; the feeling left her hands until she could no longer tell whether she held a pen or yarn and a crochet hook, making cooking dangerous because she frequently burned herself; she could no longer read her puzzle books, or even the worn Bible on the table by her rocker. In the end she moved only between her bed, the bathroom and her chair.

"I don't understand why I can't die," she said to Leon many times a day. She now knew better than to say it to the family. "I'm so tired."

But one day, after the beginning of yet another New Year, Mary said something that surprised her. When she brought in the mail and Ellen's supper after work, Mary acknowledged her mother's isolation in the sadness of her eyes, and held the shaky hands. "I know you must be lonely, Mom, sitting here with no one to talk to and nothing to do. The waiting must be hard . . . especially the waiting to die."

"No one will ever listen when I say that."

"I know, but we have to learn to let go. It's not for us to decide. I realized the other day that Dad has been gone for 25 years. That's an awfully long time to be alone."

"I feel so tired! And useless. And I know that Leon's waiting for me."

So Mary sat with her while she ate, and they listened to the television. Then she helped her into bed, turned out the lights and returned to her own home. And some time in the night, as Ellen listened to the ticking of the Regulator clock on the wall by the porch door, her breath was knocked from her lungs by a weight on her chest so heavy, so surprising, that she couldn't even call out. The room reeled and she floated free of the gasping, writhing form in the bed, toward the brilliant light. And when she reached it and could make out the form of the one who stood beyond, she stretched out her arms, smiled and sighed, "Oh, Leon!"

Mary stood alone by the coffin, patting the gnarled hand that wore the faded gold wedding band, and returned the sweet smile. She could almost hear the quavery voice whispering the words.

Author's Note: This story by Jo Perry-Sumwalt is shared in loving memory of her grandparents, Mabel and Leon Hunter.

Carrying The Cross

As they went out, they came upon a man from Cyrene named Simon; they compelled this man to carry his cross.

Matthew 27:32

One year, on Palm Sunday, I was the narrator in our church's Easter Cantata. As we were about to go into the sanctuary to sing, the pastor came up to me and asked if I would be willing to carry the cross out at the end of the service. I said yes without giving it a second thought, but as the cantata went on I had a lot of time between narrations to think about what I had been asked to do. From where I was standing I could look back and see the cross. As I thought about carrying it out, I had a strong feeling of not being worthy . . . that someone else should do it. I wondered why the pastor had asked me. Why hadn't he asked someone else? I was very much distracted from what I was supposed to be reading in the cantata. My eyes kept going back to the cross.

At the end of the service, when the pastor brought the cross over and handed it to me, I was struck by its size and weight. It wasn't a very big cross, but at that moment it seemed very large and very heavy. The walk from the front of the church to the back seemed a long way. A part of me wanted to get it over with: to get out of there and put it down, because I felt very uncomfortable with it.

When I got out into the narthex, I turned and watched as the children started to come out of the sanctuary. A little boy came over to me, looked up, touched the cross, and said, "Did Jesus really die on a cross like this?" It was all that I could do to say yes, but I did manage to get it out. I'll never forget what happened next. His face lit up as he began to comprehend, probably for the first time in his life, what Jesus had done for him.

As I lay the cross down, I felt very pleased that I had been given the opportunity to carry it.

Author's Note: Kenneth Lyerly shared this story in our District Lay Speaker's Course. It is printed here mostly in his own words. Mr. Lyerly, an alcoholism and chemical dependency counselor, lives with his family in Kenosha, Wisconsin.

Past Glory

Do not cast me off in the time of old age; do not forsake me when my strength is spent. For my enemies speak concerning me, and those who watch for my life consult together. They say, "Pursue and seize that person whom God has forsaken, for there is no one to deliver." O God, do not be far from me; O my God, make haste to help me!

Psalm 71:9-12

"Mrs. Adams!" The doctor intercepted the woman as she pushed open the front door of the Rest Haven Care Center. He'd heard that she sometimes tried to slip out early in the afternoon. She looked up, startled.

"Dr. Abrams, isn't it?" she said as he drew nearer. "Why, yes. Of course."

"I'm so happy to have caught you," he smiled down at her. "I wanted to tell you again how happy I am to be here at Rest Haven."

"Have you had a complete tour of the building yet?" she said, forgetting that she'd been on the way out.

"Yes, on my first visit," Dr. Abrams replied, supporting her elbow when she tottered slightly as they passed the empty receptionist's office on their way down the sunny hallway. She appeared not to notice.

"I've been here since the beginning, when we were still located in the old Victorian house on Hill Street. We were called a retirement home or convalescent center back then. When Mr. Adams died I took over as administrator. Now we're a skilled care facility."

The pride in her voice made him smile again. "The reputation this center is built on is well known in the area. That's why I applied here several months ago. I was very pleased when they called about the opening.''

''I think you'll find the staff very easy to get along with.'' They reached the nurses' station, the hub of six spokes which were the different wings of the center, each decorated in a different color of paint and floor tile; it was unoccupied at the moment. Mrs. Adams' sharp blue eyes ranged from the empty desk to the men and women whose wheelchairs had been lined up in front of a television in the small lounge across from it.

''These poor dears are still waiting for their afternoon naps,'' she said, stepping away from the doctor abruptly. ''Here, Frieda, your lap robe has slipped off again,'' she clucked, tucking it back in place around the drowsing woman.

''Help me!'' called a man's voice from the far end of the line. ''Please, help me!''

''Yes, Victor, the nurses will be here soon to put you to bed.''

The silver-haired doctor watched as Mrs. Adams' white head bent over those in the chairs, soothing, smoothing and quieting each one in turn. ''You still have a way with people.''

But the old woman stepped determinedly toward the green wing without any comment. After a moment's uncertainty, the doctor straightened his stooped shoulders and followed. Mrs. Adams was peering into each room.

''You tell Nurse Young I'm still good with people!'' she said.

''I'm sure she's aware. I've heard she's one of the greatest assets of this center.''

Her lips tightened. ''She probably says so! But I don't trust that woman. She's always undermining me. One day I'll prove it and she'll be on her way.''

The doctor put out his hands in entreaty. ''Surely it would be a shame to lose such a competent head nurse.'' Mrs. Adams turned away.

In the lounge which connected the green and blue wings, ambulatory residents rested in comfortable chairs, their canes and walkers nearby, and watched a soap opera or worked on a huge jigsaw puzzle. Mrs. Adams hovered over each of them, but none of them seemed to be in need.

"There's not an aide on the entire wing. Incompetents!"

Again the doctor raised a bushy eyebrow. "But you said the staff was very cooperative."

"They're a bunch of good-for-nothing loafers! You can bet they're sitting in the lounge, drinking coffee. These people need attention!"

His voice remained low and even. "May I walk you back?"

"This way!" She led him up the blue wing on the other side of the lounge, where many of the very helpless were already asleep in their beds.

Mrs. Adams' arm trembled now, beneath the doctor's hand. Back at the nurse's station there was still no sign of staff members.

"Help me!" Victor called again, "Please, I want to go to bed."

"This is inexcusable!" Mrs. Adams snapped, forging on into the red wing. Dr. Abrams had heard that when she was in one of her moods, it was best to play along. Occasional shouts and cries could be heard up and down this hallway. It was the wing for the senile and mentally unstable. The medicine cart sat by a door at the far end, but Mrs. Adams strode directly to a doorway in the middle of the hall.

"I want to thank you for your personal tour and the wonderful history of this care center," the doctor said. She just tottered into the room, sank into a chair and turned her face to the window, still trembling. At the same time, urine began to drip from the chair seat and puddle at her feet.

"Dr. Abrams, what are you doing in here?" Nurse Young said from the doorway. She consulted a chart and picked out a cup of medications from the cart behind her in the hall.

"I found her going out the front door and brought her back."

"Oh, dear. And I see that she's had an accident again." She flipped on the call light to summon a nurse's aide. "She must have been very upset. This always happens when she gets out and sees the other residents. She just can't let go.'' The head nurse gave the now docile woman her medications, securely strapped her into the chair with a restraining belt, and turned back to the doctor.

"You'd best go along now. I realize you were only trying to help, but it's best if the male residents keep out of the female residents' rooms.'' She pushed him firmly toward the door. "Mrs. Adams will be fine. You go on to your own room now and rest for a while before activities. Today is bingo, you know!''

A nurse's aide brushed past Dr. Abrams in the doorway, removing the stop so that the door began to swing shut on its own. He paused to look back at the dignified white-haired form in the chair, and just before the door closed, she turned her glaring eyes back to meet his. Her look said, "I told you so.''

Author's Note: This story was written by Jo Perry-Sumwalt.

66

The Mortician's Tale

. . . she turned around and saw Jesus standing there,
but she did not know that it was Jesus. Jesus said
to her, "Woman, why are you weeping? Whom are
you looking for?" Supposing him to be the gardener,
she said to him, "Sir, if you have carried him away,
tell me where you have laid him, and I will take him
away." Jesus said to her, "Mary." She turned and
said to him in Hebrew, "Rabboni!" (which means
Teacher). Jesus said to her, "Do not hold on to me,
because I have not yet ascended to the Father. But
go to my brothers and say to them, 'I am ascending
to my Father and your Father, to my God and your
God.' " Mary Magdalene went and announced to
the disciples, "I have seen the Lord;" and she told
them that he had said these things to her.
                                        John 20:14-18

It was on a warm Saturday afternoon, late in the spring
of 1911. I'll never forget the day. I had just returned from
my regular Saturday fishing excursion with old Doc Hallister.
We hadn't caught any fish — we rarely did — but we enjoyed
each other's company. Doctors and morticians have many
things in common. I used to kid him that my job was to bury
his mistakes, and he used to accuse me of hovering around
his office door like a vulture. This incipient black humor was
just between us: a way of coping with the stresses and tensions
of our work. He confided in me once that he had never got-
ten used to watching people die. He said it was his business
to keep people alive. That was why he had become a doctor.
He felt like a failure when death won the day. That was the
way he had put it. Young people and children, whose mothers

he had attended at their birthing, were the hardest, he said. I told him it was the same for me. Friends and the children of friends were the most difficult for me to bear. But we were both philosophical about it. These were our callings, after all: his to care for the dying, mine to prepare the dead for burial. So we went fishing every Saturday — if he wasn't out in the country somewhere delivering a baby, and if I wasn't embalming a corpse — and we talked about other things: politics and books we had read, the best tenor we had ever heard, women we had known or would like to have known, and baseball, the other great passion we shared. We were planning to take the train to Chicago to see the White Sox play in their new stadium. Cominsky Park, they called it. He never did get to go. I went with my wife a few years after he died, and I thought of him as we sat in the upper deck. Doc was a great source of comfort to me. I was glad that he was still alive after what happened on that Saturday afternoon.

As I pulled into the dooryard that day, I saw a rider bent over his horse, waiting for me under the butternut tree just beyond the gate. I pulled my rig over beside him. When he raised his head, I was able to see his face beneath the brim of his hat. It was one of Rupert Jones' boys. Rupert was a dairy farmer who lived about four miles outside of town, beyond the railroad bridge on the other side of the Little Pine River. He and I had been chums in grammar school, and we worked the railroad together when we were young bucks. We ran around together to dances and barn raisings, chased some of the same girls. He went into farming with his father after he married Pearl, and I joined Pa in the mortuary business. Rupert had asked me to be godfather for his first boy, Frank. We didn't see each other much after that. This was one of the younger ones, Earl, I think his name was.

"Pa sent me to bring you," he said. "Frank's dead — kicked by a horse this morning."

I didn't question him about the details. There was no need. It was a common occurrence in those days. I exchanged my fishing tackle for my embalming equipment, Earl tied his horse to the back of the buggy and joined me on the seat up front, and we were off. We rode in silence all the way out to the farm. Earl didn't say one word. He was in shock. I guessed that he must have been present when it happened, and I didn't try to get him to talk. It would all come out when he was ready.

The farm yard was already filled with neighbors who had come as soon as they heard. Wagons and buggies were parked all along the driveway. Some of the men had simply unhitched their work horses from the plow and ridden them across the fields. They stood in their harnesses with heads low, glad for an opportunity to rest early in the day. The men stood near their animals, speaking in quiet voices, going over the details of the accident. Small children were chasing each other around the barn. Rupert shook my hand when I got down from the buggy and thanked me for coming. He took me directly into the house, past the parlor filled with neighbor women, through the front hall and the kitchen, and onto the back porch, a lean-to room that had been added to the house as an after thought and served as a summer kitchen. It was a large, screened-in room, meant only for warm weather use. It served well for large family gatherings and as a place to feed threshing crews at harvest time. In the fall, when the air turned cold, they butchered deer and rabbits there and hung the carcasses up to cure for a few days before canning or smoking. Pearl was there with Frank's two sisters and several other women relatives. They had laid Frank's body out under a sheet on a long, hardwood table, with only his head exposed. I expressed my sympathy to Pearl, and then asked them to excuse me for a little while so that I could prepare the body. They all filed out, wiping their eyes, blowing their noses, and leaning on each other for support. The sight of me had set off a new round of weeping. It always did. I was the final harbinger of death. There was no more denying it, no more hoping that it wasn't true, after I arrived to do my work.

I pulled the sheet back and surveyed the body. There was a large red welt on the chest, but no marks on the head or face. The technical part of my job would be easy. I set myself immediately to the task at hand, trying not to let myself think too much about the life of this handsome, well-muscled young lad whose body lay before me. I would weep later, on the way home: get it all out, as I always did, before I greeted my own son. Oh, how my heart ached for Rupert and Pearl, but I put it out of my mind so I could do what I had to do. I had turned to get the needle and hose out of my bag when I heard a voice behind me speak my name.

"Mr. Cummens, is that you?"

I was startled to say the least. I turned around and there was Frank, sitting up on the edge of the table. He pulled the sheet around his body to cover himself. Then he spoke again.

"I know why you're here, and I won't interrupt you for long, but I have to tell you something before I go. Promise me you'll remember what I say. It's important that Ma and Pa hear the whole story. It will make it easier for them."

I promised him that I would listen carefully and tell them all that he said.

"Pa and I haven't been getting along," he said. "I was planning to run away and get a job in the city. I took some money out of the cash box — about $50 — just enough to get me started. I would have paid it all back. It's buried next to the big rock under the apple tree in the barnyard. I was going to leave in the morning while they were all at church. Pa probably doesn't know the money is missing yet, but he'll find out as soon as he looks in the cash box, and he'll know it was me that took it. I want you to see that he gets it back. And I want you to tell him and Ma that I am sorry for the trouble I caused them, and that I will always love them."

Then he laid his head back down on the table and was still. I stood there, numb, for a long time. I couldn't move; I couldn't even think. Finally, I forced myself to go over and touch the body. It was cold and there was no pulse. Afterward, I wasn't sure if it was Frank's ghost or Frank himself, in the flesh, who had sat up and spoken to me, but I had no doubt that it had happened. The words that he asked me to remember are forever imbedded in my memory.

The family must have wondered what was taking me so long. When I finished, at last, I bid them come in. Some of the men brought in the coffin and placed it by the table. Frank's mother and sisters would wash and dress him, and then his body would be placed in the coffin and carried into the living room for the wake that would go on all through the night and into the next day, until the time of the funeral. I would come back with the horse hearse and the preacher. My work would be complete after the procession and the burial in the cemetery. I picked up my bag of embalming equipment and the large blue bottle filled with Frank's blood, which I would dispose of later, and asked Rupert to join me outside. I walked out toward the apple tree in the barnyard with Rupert following along.When we came to the big rock, I picked up a stick and dug around until I found the package of money wrapped in a piece of old oil cloth. I gave it to Rupert, and then I told him everything that Frank had said. When I was finished, he grabbed me and hugged me to his big farmer frame so hard that I thought for sure he had broken several of my ribs. Then he turned, without saying a word, and went back into the house.

When I had finished repeating the story to old Doc, as we sat fishing on the bank of the Little Pine the following Saturday morning, he leaned back against a log, blew a big puff of smoke from his pipe, and said, "I'll be damned. Maybe death doesn't win!"

Author's Note: This story is shared in loving memory of Eleanor Cummings Steinhaus, who was a funeral director, with her husband Carl, in Montello, Wisconsin, from 1947 to 1976. They inherited the business from her father, C.A. Cummings, who founded it in 1905.

Opening The Scriptures

*When he was at the table with them, he took bread,
blessed and broke it, and gave it to them. Then their
eyes were opened, and they recognized him; and he
vanished from their sight. They said to each other,
"Were not our hearts burning within us while he was
talking to us on the road, while he was opening the
scriptures to us?"*

Luke 24:30-32

My dad was ill for a long time with heart disease and emphysema. He suffered several heart attacks and was hospitalized frequently. I had never felt the same kind of closeness
between us that I believed he shared with my younger brother,
who was an engineer like Dad. I don't think that Dad ever
really understood the counseling and behavioral sciences that
I had made my life's work. And he had never been a very
demonstrative person when it came to sharing emotions. He
had always given of himself and his talents instead. Dad was
a self-educated, self-made man who held up education to us
as one of the most vital things in life. He was our living exam-
ple. During my most recent visit, I had told Dad how much
I loved him — how much he meant to me, and my fears about
his dying — but he wasn't ready to deal with the possibility
of death and denied that he was gravely ill. I had to put my
fingers to his lips to quiet him so I could finish what I had
to say, because I needed him to know those things before it
was too late. It was a way of preparing myself for his eventual
death.

When my mother called the last time to tell us that Dad
was in the hospital again, and not doing well, I knew we had
to go home. I wanted to be there with him and Mom. The

doctor let us know right away that Dad wouldn't make it out of the hospital this time. I sat by his bed, holding his hand as he struggled with great pain. At night I prayed that God would take him soon, for Mom's sake as well as Dad's, because I could tell how hard it was for her to see him suffer. We were with him when he died the next day, and his last words to each of us were, "I love you." I don't remember more than two other times in my whole life when he said that to me.

As we talked with the pastor about the service, I told him that I felt a very strong need to speak at Dad's funeral. His illness had caused memory lapses, bluntness, and sometimes even cruelty in his relationships with family and friends, and I don't want people to be left with that impression of him. I wanted everyone to remember him as I did. For two days I struggled with what I would say. I wanted to express how much Dad meant to me, and I wanted it to be perfect . . . a trait I had inherited from him. I studied several scripture passages, hoping for an inspiration, but my mind was blocked and time was running short. Finally I tossed the Bible onto the bed and took a break.

When I returned to the bedroom later, still struggling with my thoughts, I saw my father sitting on the bed, and I heard a voice say, "It's okay." It was a brief sensation: natural and not frightening at all. I walked over and picked up the Bible, which had fallen open to Proverbs when I tossed it onto the bed. The passage read:

> *Listen, children, to a father's instruction, and be attentive, that you may gain insight; for I give you good precepts: do not forsake my teaching. When I was a son with my father, tender, and my mother's favorite, he taught me, and said to me, "Let your heart hold fast my words; keep my commandments, and live."*
> — Proverbs 4:1-5

This scripture opened to me the memories of my father that I cherished the most . . . his self-education; how he had risen from being a grade school dropout to hold an engineer's position before he retired; his love of books, and the way he had encouraged us to learn. These were the things I wanted others to know and remember about him. They were the thoughts and memories I would share the next day.

Later that night, my father's oldest, dearest friend stopped by to see us. In the course of the conversation, he said that he hoped no one would try to speak at the funeral, because he didn't think he could stand it. I didn't say anything about my plans. But after the funeral he thanked me for sharing. He agreed that those things had needed to be said. I sensed that I had succeeded in giving my father back some of what he had given to me.

Author's Note: This story, related to the author by Kenneth Lyerly, is shared in loving memory of his father, Eddie Lyerly.

When Peace Came

When it was evening on that day, the first day of the week, and the doors of the house where the disciples had met were locked for fear of the Jews, Jesus came and stood among them and said, "Peace be with you."

John 20:19

The day my brother-in-law Dick died we were all gathered around his hospital bed. His children had arrived, and when they had said their goodbyes and he was at peace with himself, Dick died very quickly and quietly. His struggle with heart and lung disease had been long and painful, but he was prepared to die: more prepared one of the nuns said, than she had ever seen anyone. And I knew the day his peace of mind and acceptance had begun.

For more than a week, my wife Betty and I had been making daily trips from Kenosha to Milwaukee to visit Dick during his final stay in the hospital. Over the years he had gone through bypass surgery, a valve replacement and a pacemaker implant, but his condition, complicated even further by asbestosis, continued to deteriorate. His system reacted against the volumes of medication he was required to take, and he was hospitalized again and again to regulate it. Part of our reason for returning to Wisconsin from Alabama was the knowledge that he didn't have much longer to live. We wanted to be close enough to see him regularly — to be there for him and Betty's sister, Virginia. But that particular day Betty and I were both very tired after work, and we couldn't face the drive to Milwaukee. We decided that we would rest up and visit again the next day.

After dinner I began to feel a very strong sense of *needing* to go see Dick. I didn't hear any voices speaking to me, but something inside was urging me to see him. Betty was surprised when I told her we were going after all, but I never questioned the urge. I just said we needed to go.

When we walked into the hospital, we met Virginia coming down from Dick's room, and she was very upset. We spent some time with her in the chapel, and she let down her defenses and cried. Virginia is a very strong person, and that was the first time she had leaned on us for support. Then we went up to Dick's room.

We don't always love, or even like, those people who become a part of our family through marriage. But Dick and I always got along, and he had become especially important to me when my son, John, was having some problems. I took him for counseling and the psychologist suggested that we needed some time apart. He asked if there was anyone we knew who lived on a farm where John might stay for a while, so I called Dick and he took him in for a few months. I had a great fear at that time that I might lose John to him, but Dick in his loving way returned John to me. It made a great difference in the relationship between John and all of our family, and I never forgot Dick's willingness to help.

In spite of our special relationship, walking into his hospital room that night was very difficult. I didn't really want to be there. My father had died of emphysema the year before, and Dick was required to inhale the same kind of medication Dad had been on as he lay dying. Just the smell of it made me want to turn around and leave. But when Dick saw us come through the door he said he'd been praying all day that I would come.

As I sat there, listening while Dick spoke of his impending death for the first time, there was a part of me that wanted to run, and I might have if Dick hadn't been holding my hand. It must have showed, because I remember Betty asking if I was okay, and I knew I was, in spite of everything. I was very much aware that I wasn't there by my own choice — my own decision making, but because Dick needed me. Dealing with people in grief is part of my job as a counselor, but I wasn't there to counsel Dick. I was there because I loved him, and

76

because I had obeyed the sense of urgency I felt. He needed someone to hear his thoughts on death, and he trusted me to be that person. I don't see having gone as a choice. I didn't want to be there, in that room, with the smell of medication that reminded me of my father's death. Maybe I even feared that Dick might die while I held his hand, as my father had. And yet their deaths were so very different. Dad fought death as long as he could. He wasn't prepared to die. Dick met his death, dealt with it and died ready, with a grace and peace I'll never forget.

Dick clearly entered a new stage in his development and his relationship to others when he talked about his death that night. And it affected me, too. In his dying, Dick gave me a most unexpected gift: a peace that will stay with me as long as I live.

Author's Note: This story, told to the author by Kenneth Lyerly, is shared in loving memory of Dick Hill.

A Pretty Little Room

Do not let your hearts be troubled. Believe in God, believe also in me. In my Father's house there are many dwelling places. If it were not so, would I have told you that I go to prepare a place for you? And if I go and prepare a place for you, I will come again and will take you to myself, so that where I am, there you may be also.

John 14:1-3

The old woman, cold and wet in her layers of outdoor clothes, was sure the room before her must be one of those open-eye dreams she had. She remembered having felt drowsy earlier, but what she saw now was too real to be a sleeping-dream.

"You gonna run me off from here?" she said gruffly to the man in the room. If this was an open-eye dream he probably wasn't really there, anyway.

"No, Mary, this room is all yours. No one will run you off."

She looked at him sharply. No one had called her Mary for 20 years, maybe more. She wanted to ask him how he knew to call her that, but the heat radiating from the little oil burner by the rocking chair was drawing her into the room.

"Such a pretty little room," she sighed, touching the crocheted afghan on the rocker's back as she stretched frostbitten fingers out over the stove's warmth. "I used to have a room years . . . years ago. I had me some things in it, too. Whose room did you say this is?"

The man's face looked somehow softer, less masculine, now. "Your room, Mary. You can stay here from now on."

"Old Marguerite and Crazy Eddie would bust a gut to see me in this room!" Mary laughed and laughed, then suddenly

78

stopped. "Where are they, now, anyway? How did I get here?" Frightened, she tried to remember what had happened before she came to herself in this room.

"Gotta go inside tonight," Old Marguerite had said yesterday. "Cold is comin'. Real cold."

"I ain't goin' inside," Mary said out loud to the memory of Old Marguerite. "They ask too many questions inside. Want to know what's nobody's business. They take my things away inside, and people are too close together. I ain't goin'. Besides, if real cold is comin', won't be no room anyhow."

Mary jumped as the open-eye dream ended, surprised to still find herself in the warmth of the little room. Her four big department store shopping bags were lined neatly along the wall by a bureau to the left of the door. There were pictures of people hanging on the flowered wallpaper above them, and when she squinted at the faces they seemed familiar.

"Old Marguerite and Crazy Eddie went to the shelters and the hospitals tryin' to get inside last night. I got inside once, in a hospital, and thought I'd never get out again. They took my things away in there, called me by the wrong name, and treated me like I was crazy. I get open-eye dreams sometimes, but I ain't never been crazy."

She touched the rocking chair again. "I had me a little rockin' chair like this, once, that sat by a oil stove. Used to put my feet up after work and listen to my radio. I hocked that chair and that radio when I got fired from my store cleanin' job in 1965. Wasn't more than 55 then, but nobody would hire me again. Lived mostly on the street ever since the landlord kicked me out of my little room. Hocked most all my things."

A movement by the door brought Mary back to the present. "You can put your things away here in this room," said the woman standing there. "You can unpack to stay."

Mary's glance fell on the old, red velvet sofa on the woman's right. It was the kind that laid out flat to make a bed, and somehow she knew that if she lifted the front her pillow, crisp white sheets and blue patchwork quilt would be in the storage compartment below.

"How did I get to this room?" She looked all around it again. "I remember gatherin' newspapers out of trashbins and pullin' that old cardboard down the alley over a manhole cover. I put on all the clothes I had, with my big coat over the top, and a pair of boots I found in a dumpster." She looked down in awe at the black shoes, cotton stockings, print dress and apron she was wearing now. "I packed all the newspapers around me, but I remember bein'cold . . . never so cold before in all my life . . . ."

Mary paused, walked to the window, raised the shade and looked down on a frozen alleyway far below. She could just make out her heavy, men's boots sticking out of one end of a cardboard tent in the snow. A thermometer out on the windowsill read 31 degrees below zero.

Now Mary knew where she was. She no longer spoke, but moved about the pretty little room, hanging some family pictures from her shopping bags on empty nails among the other pictures on the wall, restoring chipped and cracked knickknacks to their places on the bureau, making up the sofa bed with her pillow, crisp sheets and blue patchwork quilt. Then she lowered herself tentatively into the rocker next to the warm stove. The figure in the doorway, no longer male or female, but a hazy, benevolent presence, faded away, as did everything beyond the bounds of the four comforting walls. Mary sighed and smiled as she put her feet up and switched on the radio.

Author's Note: This story was written by Jo Perry-Sumwalt.

Creation

*In the beginning when God created the heavens and
the earth, the earth was a formless void and darkness covered the face of the deep . . .*
Genesis 1:1-2b

The Almighty One was alone. There was empty darkness
as far as far could be, in every direction; up, down, under,
around, out and beyond — nothingness: a great colorless void.
Suddenly the Almighty One exploded. She could contain herself no longer. Worlds and suns went out in every direction.
A whole universe was born in an instant. Galaxies of bright,
shining stars twinkled in the darkness. The great void was filled
with light.

"My, my," the Almighty One thought, "what a lovely
sight." And she sat and looked at what she had created, and
looked and looked until she had seen all that her almighty eyes
could see. "It is not finished," she thought. "Something more
is needed. I wonder if, perhaps, it might be possible . . . ."
And as the Almighty One pondered the possibilities, here and
there, on some of the worlds, life began to form. Rain fell,
cells divided, seeds sprouted, plants grew, eggs hatched; creatures began to swim and crawl and run and dance before the
Almighty One's eyes. "It is good," she thought. "Yes, it is
good. I shall let them live and grow and take care of all my
worlds. And when they are ready we will . . . ah, but that is
enough for now."

And then the Almighty One smiled inside of herself and
heaved a great sigh of relief. She was no longer alone.

The Best Mama

A capable wife who can find? She is far more precious than jewels. The heart of her husband trusts in her and he will have no lack of gain . . .

She looks well to the ways of her household, and does not eat the bread of idleness. Her children rise up and call her happy; her husband too, and he praises her: "Many women have done excellently, but you surpass them all." Charm is deceitful, and beauty is vain, but a woman who fears the Lord is to be praised. Give her a share in the fruit of her hands, and let her works praise her in the city gates.
Proverbs 31:10-11, 27-31

There was once a little girl who loved her mama with all of her heart. At night, when her mama tucked her into bed, she would throw her arms around her, kiss her on both cheeks and say, "You're the best mama in the whole wide world."

When Mother's Day came, the little girl decided to get her mama a nice present to show how much she loved her. She thought and thought and thought about what she could give her. One day she went with her papa to the corner store and there in the window she saw the perfect gift. It was a tiny crystal bell which tinkled ever so softly, like the wind chimes that hung outside the kitchen window. How lovely it would look in mama's china cabinet in the corner of the parlor. Her papa helped her buy the bell, and he told her to hide it away carefully 'til Mother's Day. The little girl wrapped the crystal bell in tissue paper and tucked it away in the back of her sock drawer. Mama would never find it there.

When Mother's Day came, the little girl opened the sock drawer, took out the bell, unwrapped it carefully from the tissue paper, and was about to ring it one last time before giving it to her mama when it slipped out of her fingers, crashed to the floor and shattered into a hundred pieces. The little girl was heartbroken. Now what would she give her mama to show her how much she loved her? She began to cry, and she ran to her mama saying, "I had a nice present to give you for Mother's Day, but it broke and now I don't have anything to give you."

"There, there," Mama said, as she wiped her daughter's tears, "You have already given me the best present possible. What I want more than anything else is to know that you love me."

Upon hearing this, the little girl stopped crying and began to smile. Then she gave her mama a big hug, kissed her on both cheeks, and you know what she said. "You're the best mama in the whole wide world."

That little girl is grown up now, and she has a daughter and a granddaughter and a little great-granddaughter of her own. She is almost 100 years old, and she lives in a nursing home. Every Mother's Day her daughter and her granddaughter and her little great-granddaughter come to the nursing home — and they put their arms around her and kiss her on both cheeks, and you know what they say . . .

Author's Note: This story is dedicated to Bernice Long Sumwalt, who will always be, for me, the best mama in the whole wide world.

Before A Fall

Everyone who hears these words of mine and acts on them will be like a wise man who built his house on rock. The rain fell, the floods came, and the winds blew and beat on that house, but it did not fall, because it had been founded on rock. And everyone who hears these words of mine and does not act on them will be like a foolish man who built his house on sand. The rain fell, and the floods came, and the winds blew and beat against that house, and it fell — and great was its fall!

Matthew 7:24-27

Two boys were building sand castles on the beach beside the ocean. Both built very fine castles with beautiful towers, turrets, moats and bridges. When they were finished, each boy in turn stepped back to admire his work. Both boys were very pleased with themselves.

The first boy went up and down the beach calling out for everyone to come and see his castle. When people came to look, he proudly pointed to his work and said, "I build the best sand castles in the world." Everyone admitted it was one of the finest sand castles they had ever seen. The first boy beamed and held his head up high.

A small girl came by and asked if he would show her how to build a sand castle. "Oh, no," said the first little boy, "I couldn't show you. My technique is a secret. If I show you, you might show someone else, and before long everyone would know how to build fine sand castles, and I would no longer be the best sand castle builder in the world."

The little girl hung her head and walked away sadly. Soon all of his admirers were gone, and the first little boy was left alone. When the tide came in and washed his sand castle away, he cried and vowed never to build another sand castle.

The second boy, after admiring his sand castle, began immediately to build another. As people came by and commented on the beauty of his work, he invited them to join him. Soon there was a happy throng of castle builders all around him, including the little girl who had been turned away by the first boy. When the tide came in and washed their sand castles away, they all laughed and began to build bigger and better castles a little higher up on the beach.

Rudi The Restless Rooster

*Are not two sparrows sold for a penny? Yet not one
of them will fall to the ground apart from your
Father. And even the hairs of your head are all
counted. So do not be afraid; you are of more value
than many sparrows.*

Matthew 10:29-31

There was once a young, restless rooster named Rudi who
could not sleep at night. Long after all the other chickens in
the coop had climbed up onto the roost, said their good nights
and nodded off to dreamland, Rudi would be awake, pacing
up and down, too afraid to go to sleep. Rudi was afraid of
the dark, and so he would stay up all night long, watching and
listening lest something jump out of the dark and grab him.
The least little noise would scare him out of his wits. Whenever
he heard a twig fall to the ground, or the wind blowing in the
tree branches, Rudi would be certain that a fox or weasel was
coming to get him. One night when an owl hooted outside the
window, he flew up to the top of the coop and refused to come
down for three days.

The other chickens soon grew weary of Rudi's tiresome,
restless behavior. Finally, one day, one of the old roosters took
him aside for a rooster-to-rooster talk. He threw one of his
great wings around Rudi and said, "Now, look here my boy,
we can't have you waking up the hens at all hours of the night.
They need their rest so they can lay plenty of eggs. You know
if they don't lay enough eggs the farmer will chop off all of
our heads. Now, what's the problem? Why can't you go to
sleep at night like a good rooster should?"

"Don't you know," whined Rudi, "that there are weasels
and foxes and bears out there when it's dark? I'm afraid they're
going to get me."

86

"Have you ever seen one?" asked the old rooster.

"No," admitted Rudi, "I've never seen one, but I know that they're out there."

"Well, they've never bothered any of the rest of us," said the old rooster. "And besides," he added, "God takes care of us."

"How do you know that?" asked Rudi.

"It says so in the Bible," said the old rooster. "Look here." And he opened the Bible to the gospel of Matthew and began to read:

> *Are not two sparrows sold for a penny? Yet not one of them will fall to the ground apart from your father. And even the [feathers] of your head are all counted. So do not be afraid; you are of more value than many sparrows.*

"You see," said the old rooster, "God is watching over us. We don't have to be afraid."

Rudi thought and thought about what the old rooster had said. And that night, when all of the chickens climbed up on the roost and said their goodnights before nodding off into chicken dreamland, Rudi was the first one to fall asleep. They never called him Rudi the Restless Rooster again.

Learning To Pray

Likewise the Spirit helps us in our weakness; for we do not know how to pray as we ought, but that very Spirit intercedes with sighs too deep for words. And God who searches the heart, knows what is the mind of the Spirit, because the Spirit intercedes for the Saints according to the will of God.
Romans 8:26-27

There was once a little boy who did not know how to pray. He asked one of his friends about it one day, and his friend said, "It is really very easy. Each night you must kneel down beside your bed and say, 'God bless Mommy, God bless Daddy and God bless me. Amen.' That is all there is to it." The little boy tried it that night, but somehow it didn't seem to be enough. "There must be more to prayer than this," he thought.

The next morning at breakfast, he asked his mom to show him how to pray. "But you know how to pray," his mom told him. "Just fold your hands, close your eyes and say, 'Dear God, please bless this food that we are about to eat.' " The little boy prayed as his mother said, but that didn't seem to be enough either.

That same afternoon, he asked his father to show him how to pray. "It is very simple," his father said, "When you wish to pray, go into a church, bow your head and say, 'Thank you God for all the blessings of life.' " The next time they were in church, the little boy prayed as his father said, but still he wasn't sure that he really knew how to pray. Something was lacking. He was sure that there must be something more about prayer: something crucial that they had forgotten to teach him.

That very night his grandmother came to visit. After supper, when they were alone, the little boy climbed up onto her lap and said, "Grandma, will you teach me how to pray? I know all about kneeling down beside my bed, and folding my hands and bowing my head. I even know some of the right words to say. But, still, I wonder if I really and truly know how to pray."

His grandmother smiled and said, "I think you are ready to learn about the most important part of prayer . . . listening to God."

"What do you mean?" the little boy asked. "What should I listen for? Does God talk back? What does God say? How will I know God is talking to me?"

"Shhhhh," his grandmother said. "You will know. Just listen." And so the two of them sat very quietly together and began to listen.

Don't Forget Your Lunch

"We have nothing here but five loaves and two fish." And he said, "Bring them here to me." Then he ordered the crowds to sit down on the grass. Taking the five loaves and the two fish, he looked up to heaven, and blessed and broke the loaves, and gave them to the disciples, and the disciples gave them to the crowds. And all ate and were filled; and they took up what was left over of the broken pieces, twelve baskets full. And those who ate were about five thousand men, besides women and children.

Matthew 14:17b-21

A little boy came running into the house one day, yelling, "Mom, Mom, Jesus is coming. Everyone is going to see him. May I go, too?"

"Yes, you may go," his mother said, "but be sure to wear your heavy cloak. It might get cold later in the day. And don't forget your lunch. I fixed you some nice fish and fresh bread."

"Awe, Mom," the little boy said, "nobody else is taking a lunch. It is just for a little while. I don't want to carry my lunch around all day. Besides, I don't like fish."

"You take it," his mother said. "There is no telling when you will get back to the house. You will be starving in a couple of hours. Maybe you could trade your fish for some nice goat cheese."

The little boy reluctantly took his lunch and ran off to join the crowd that was gathering around Jesus. The day lasted much longer than he expected, and before long he was very hungry, just as his mother had predicted. Even the fish looked good. He was just about to take a bite when he heard some of Jesus' disciples asking if anyone had any food that they

90

would be willing to share. He quickly held up his hand and called out, "Over here! I've got five loaves and two fish."

The little boy watched as the disciples took the fish and the bread to Jesus. He watched to see what Jesus was going to do. Jesus simply took the bread and fish, blessed them, and somehow everyone got fed, including the little boy who ended up with (guess what?) somebody else's goat cheese.

Leonardo The Lonely Squirrel

Jesus left that place and went away to the district of Tyre and Sidon. Just then a Canaanite woman from that region came out and started shouting, "Have mercy on me, Lord, Son of David; my daughter is tormented by a demon." But he did not answer her at all. And his disciples came and urged him, saying, "Send her away, for she keeps shouting after us." He answered, "I was sent only to the lost sheep of the house of Israel." But she came and knelt before him saying, "Lord, help me." He answered, "It is not fair to take the children's food and throw it to the dogs." She said, "Yes, Lord, yet even the dogs eat the crumbs that fall from their master's table." Then Jesus answered her, "Woman, great is your faith! Let it be done for you as you wish." And her daughter was healed instantly.

Matthew 15:21-28

Once upon a time, in the land of gray squirrels, there lived a little red squirrel named Leonardo. There were many little gray squirrels, and they had a wonderful time chasing each other about from tree to tree, but Leonardo was the only little red squirrel in the whole forest. Everyday he watched the little gray squirrels playing together, and he wished that he had someone to play with, too. But, alas, the little gray squirrels never invited him to play with them.

Leonardo became very lonely. It is no fun to play all by yourself. So, one day he scampered up to the little gray squirrels and asked if he could play with them. They took one look at him and said, "Sorry Red, you're the wrong color. We only play with gray squirrels. Go away, you're bothering us."

92

"Oh yeah?" said Leonardo. "We'll see about that!" Before the little gray squirrels could blink, he ran up the tree they had been playing in and called out over his shoulder, "Catch me if you can!" Without stopping to think about what color he was, the gray squirrels took off after him. They chased him all afternoon and didn't give up until they heard their mothers calling them to come home to supper. By that time they had forgotten about Leonardo's color. They just wanted to catch him. "We'll catch you tomorrow," they called out as they headed for home.

Leonardo smiled. He wasn't lonely anymore.

Preaching To The Choir

So the last will be first, and the first will be last.
Matthew 20:16

Boyd Dillard joined the chancel choir on his 75th birthday, a week after he became a member of the church. He had been an active barbershopper for years and he belonged to the local chorus guild, but this was his first experience in a church choir. His rich baritone voice was a welcome addition, and he readily joined in the merriment and camaraderie enjoyed by the men in the back row bass section.

Ann Hershner joined the choir in late October, shortly before the start of Christmas cantata rehearsals. She had just moved to town from out of state to take a position in the music department at the local college. Several choir members commented on her beautiful alto voice at the end of her first practice and told her how glad they were to have her in their group.

The very next week, the choir director handed out the music for the Christmas cantata. It was an old, familiar work, much loved by everyone. The director then announced who would be singing the solos and their special parts. Boyd and Ann were to sing a duet which everyone recognized to be the key musical climax in the cantata. Both Ann and Boyd seemed pleased to be chosen for these important parts, but no one else was smiling. "It's not fair!" someone was heard to mutter down at the end of the alto section. "She just joined the choir. Why should she get to sing the best part?" There was also some grumbling among the men in the parking lot later, after Boyd had gone home. "It's not right," one of the tenors said. "Some of us have been singing in the church choir for years and years. I think we should be shown some consideration."

The following week, as the choir director was about to begin rehearsal, Harold Rehburg asked if he might be permitted to lead the choir in a brief devotion before they started to sing. Harold was the choir's senior member. Only a few months earlier they had celebrated his 50th anniversary with the chancel choir. The director nodded his assent, and everyone waited expectantly to hear what it was that Harold had to share. He opened his Bible to the 20th chapter of Matthew and began to read:

For the kingdom of heaven is like a landowner who went out early in the morning to hire laborers for his vineyard. After agreeing with the laborers for the usual daily wage, he sent them into his vineyard. When he went out about nine o'clock, he saw others standing idle in the market-place; and he said to them, "You also go into the vine-yard, and I will pay you whatever is right." So they went. When he went out again about noon and about three o'clock, he did the same. And about five o'clock he went out and found others standing around; and he said to them, "Why are you standing here idle all day?" They said to him, "Because no one has hired us." He said to them, "You also go into the vineyard." When evening came, the owner of the vineyard said to his manager, "Call the laborers and give them their pay, beginning with the last and then going to the first." When those hired about five o'clock came, each of them received the usual daily wage. Now when the first came, they thought they would receive more; but each of them also received the usual daily wage. And when they received it, they grum-bled against the landowner, saying, "These last worked only one hour, and you have made them equal to us who have borne the burden of the day and the scorching heat." But he replied to one of them, "Friend, I am do-ing you no wrong; did you not agree with me for the usual daily wage? Take what belongs to you and go. I choose to give to this last the same as I give to you. Am I not allowed to do what I choose with what belongs to me? Or are you envious because I am generous?" So the last will be first and the first will be last.

Author's Note: This story is shared in honor of Harold Rehberg, who has been singing in the tenor section of the Cargill United Methodist Chancel Choir in Janesville, Wisconsin for more than 50 years.

What Counts In The End?

What do you think? A man had two sons; he went to the first and said, "Son, go and work in the vineyard today." He answered, "I will not;" but later he changed his mind and went. The father went to the second and said the same; and he answered, "I go, sir;" but he did not go. Which of the two did the will of his father?

Matthew 21:28-31

There was once a woman who believed very strongly in the sanctity of marriage. She had twin daughters, and as they grew up, she tried to impress on them the importance of fidelity in the marriage relationship.

When the girls reached their 18th birthday, she asked them to promise her that when they married, they would always be faithful to their husbands.

The first daughter said, "Why, certainly, Mother, I promise that when I marry it will be for life, and I will always be faithful to my husband."

The second daughter said, "Oh, no, I could never make a promise like that. Life is too uncertain. I want to be free to do what I need to do."

Not long after this, both daughters met young men and fell in love. The first daughter became engaged and had a big, formal wedding in a downtown church, with 12 attendants, three flower girls and a seven-piece brass ensemble. In the traditional words of the high church service, she promised her groom that she would love, comfort, honor, in sickness and in health, forsake all others and keep only unto him as long as they both lived.

In less than three months they were divorced and she was running around with another man.

The second daughter moved in with the man she loved, and she lived with him several years without the benefit of marriage. When they decided to have children, they went to the courthouse and were married in a simple civil ceremony. They had six children and lived happily together for 60 years.

Which of these two daughters did the will of the mother?

Who May Come To The Banquet

A Sermon With Three Stories

*Once more Jesus spoke to them in parables saying:
"The kingdom of heaven may be compared to a king
who gave a wedding banquet for his son. He sent
his slaves to call those who had been invited to the
wedding banquet, but they would not come. Again
he sent other slaves, saying, 'Tell those who have
been invited: Look, I have prepared my dinner, my
oxen and my fatted calves have been slaughtered,
and everything is ready; come to the wedding banquet.' But they made light of it and went away, one
to his farm, another to his business, while the rest
seized his slaves, mistreated them, and killed them.
The king was enraged. He sent his troops, destroyed
those murderers, and burned their city. Then he said
to his slaves, 'The wedding is ready, but those invited were not worthy. Go therefore into the main
streets, and invite everyone you find to the wedding
banquet.' Those slaves went out into the streets and
gathered all whom they found, both good and bad;
so the wedding hall was filled with guests.*

*"But when the king came in to see the guests,
he noticed a man there who was not wearing a wedding robe, and he said to him, 'Friend, how did you
get in here without a wedding robe?' And he was
speechless. Then the king said to his attendants,
'Bind him hand and foot, and throw him into the
outer darkness where there will be weeping and
gnashing of teeth.' For many are called, but few are
chosen."*

Matthew 22:1-14

How many of you would pick this parable as your favorite Bible story? Is it anyone's favorite parable? It doesn't even make the top 10, does it?

Did you notice that this parable about a wedding banquet is different from the parable of the Great Banquet which is found in Luke? That's the one we sing the song about . . .

I cannot come to the banquet, don't bother me now,
I have married a wife, I have bought me a cow.
I have fields and commitments that cost a pretty sum.
Pray hold me excused, I cannot come.

That's the one we like! The invited guests won't come, and so the host sends the servants out into the streets and lanes of the city to bring in the poor and maimed and blind and lame, but none of those who were invited are allowed to taste the banquet. It appeals to our sense of justice. We can imagine ourselves among those who have previously been excluded from great banquets *finally* getting our rightful place at the table.

The Wedding Banquet, Retold

But this parable of the wedding banquet is different. Those invited to the banquet not only refuse to come, they make light of the invitation and they kill the slaves who delivered it. So the king sends his soldiers (his terminators) and has them destroyed. Then he sends his slaves out into the streets to invite everyone else they can find. And the slaves go out and bring in both the good and the bad, until the wedding hall is filled. So far, so good: except this one gets a PG-13 rating for violence (Close your eyes, kids, don't look. It gets worse.). When the king comes in to see the guests, he notices this one poor working stiff who isn't wearing a coat and tie. And he says, "How did you get in here without a coat and tie?" And the poor slob is speechless! How was he supposed to know there was a dress code? And where was he going to get a coat and tie on short notice? They said come, there's gonna be a party and free food, so he had come! The king shows no mercy. He says to his terminators: "Bind him hand and foot, and throw him into the outer darkness, where there will be weeping and gnashing of teeth."

Jonathan Edwards must have liked to quote this text when he preached those "sinners in the hands of an angry God" sermons: "Bind him hand and foot and throw him into the outer darkness where there will be weeping and gnashing of teeth."

It has a nice ring to it, doesn't it?

I wonder how people responded when Jesus first told this story? Did they walk out on him? Did they stay to hear more stories? I wonder how we would respond if he told it here, to us?

There is a large segment of our right-brained, academic, scientific, business-oriented, corporate America that doesn't like stories very much — some who are downright hostile to stories and storytellers.

When I tell people I am a storyteller, they always assume I tell stories to children (which is true, I do tell stories to children). But when I tell them that most of my stories are for adults, they don't know how to respond. We have been taught, in this age of science and reason, that stories are for kids. Don't tell *me* any stories, we say. Tell me the truth! "Don't story me." Especially not in church! We want to hear real Bible-preaching when we come to church. We want *real* preaching, like Jesus did. "Bind him hand and foot and throw him into the outer darkness . . ."

We don't like this story very much. It offends our sense of fairness and justice, like some of those other stories he told — *The Laborers in the Vineyard* and *The Unjust Steward*. Judgment and condemnation is not what we want to hear, especially at a service of Holy Communion. We want to hear about love and forgiveness and *Amazing Grace* and *The Bread of Life for All is Broken*. It is, isn't it? That's what we've always believed. That's why we are here.

So, what are we to do with this story?

Frankly, if it had been up to me, I wouldn't have selected it for this service today. I didn't want to preach on it. I did everything I could do to avoid it, and I have, until now. But here it is, and it is in the Bible, after all — and Jesus did tell it, so what are we going to do? We might as well live with it.

If we are to believe Jesus here, it would seem that God is very particular about who comes to the banquet. But then, so are we particular, not only about who may be served at the banquet table, but who we will allow to serve.

Is everyone welcome at the banquet table in the church where you worship? How about little children? There are a great many Christian churches where children are not permitted to come to the Lord's table until they are old enough to understand what communion means.

My Uncle Max was retarded, and he lived to be 58 years old. He never grew old enough to understand the meaning of communion. I doubt that he was ever confirmed. But I think he probably had a better sense of the holy — a discernment of the body of Christ, as Paul calls it — than many of the rest of us in the family who matured beyond the seven-year-old mentality he attained.

Some churches don't even allow children to worship with adults. Never mind that Jesus said, "Suffer the little children to come to me." They rush them off to children's church or Sunday school immediately after the children's sermon. We can't expect kids to sit still that long, we say. They might disturb the rest of us in our holy communion.

Through The Ice

When we lived in Montello, a little county seat town near Wisconsin Dells, about 60 miles north of Madison, in Wisconsin, and had been there about five years, the congregation built a new church. We moved in in November, and then in early December we had an open house so that everyone in the community could come and see our new building. About half-way through the afternoon, I received an emergency phone call. Two of the little girls from our congregation had been playing out on the ice on one of the local lakes, and had fallen through. By the time I got to the hospital I knew that they had been under the water for 45 minutes, and when they brought them up they were not breathing, and their hearts were not beating. I found their grandfather in the hospital chapel, praying. This was the grandfather who brought them to worship every Sunday. You can guess what he was praying . . . "Dear God, if it be thy will, take this old man, and let my little girls live."

We finally got word that the doctors had revived both of them, and were told that they were strong enough that they could be transferred by Med-Flight to the trauma center at University Hospital in Madison. We drove down there, and we waited and prayed, until at last one of the doctors came in to tell us that they were both stable. I went home to wait some more and to pray with the congregation that was gathering that night for the annual Christmas program.

The girls were in critical care for several days. We were told that their chances of surviving were good. But on Christmas day, as our family was getting ready to open Christmas presents, we received word that Jessica, the five-year-old, had died. It was a sad Christmas for everyone in our little congregation. We had the first funeral in our new church building. But I was comforted by one image that stays with me until this day: that of Jessica and her seven-year-old sister, Candy, kneeling at the communion rail with their grandfather on the Sunday before they went through the ice.

———————

How about the gay and lesbian persons in your community? Are they allowed to come to the banquet? Practicing gays and lesbians? Would you kneel beside a homosexual person and break the bread of life with him or her, and share the covenant cup? Would you take the bread and cup from your pastor if you knew that he or she was one of the thousands of practicing pastors and priests who are gays and lesbians?

We are very particular about who may come to the banquet, and we are even more particular about who we will permit to serve us!

If God is particular about who may come to the banquet, and we are particular about who we will eat and drink with at the banquet table, who may come?

Jesus said, "Blessed are you who are hungry, for you will be filled (Luke 5:21)."

Are you hungry?

Come of you are hungry. And if you have been given living bread to share, come and serve.

I want to leave you with a story:

The Boy Who Had Everything

There was once a little boy who had everything. At least he thought he had everything. He lived in a big, beautiful house, with a swimming pool and a tree house in the backyard. He had a 10-speed bike, a go-cart and an all-terrain vehicle in the garage, all of which he could ride any time he pleased. In his bedroom he had a 27-inch color television, a VCR, a stereo, a compact disc player, a computer, a Nintendo, and dozens of movies and video games. He even had his own telephone and answering machine.

So on Saturday and Sunday mornings, the boy who had everything, played all alone with all of his wonderful things. Sometimes he and his dad would go biking, or would ride their all-terrain vehicles down at the beach. In the afternoons he went shopping at the mall with his mom and dad, and they bought more wonderful things. Somehow it never seemed to be enough. He had a hunger, deep down inside himself, for something else. He wasn't sure what it was that he was hungry for, but he knew it was something he didn't have.

The boy who lived next door to the boy who had everything didn't have nearly as many nice things. He lived in a modest house with a small backyard which had barely enough room for his tire swing and sand box. He had a three-speed bike and a red wagon in his garage, and in his room there was a cage with his pet hamster, his baseball card collection, his comic books, and a wall covered with posters. He also had a dog named Rex who knew how to roll over and play dead.

On Saturdays the boy next door played catch with his dad in the backyard. In the afternoon, sometimes, his mom would fix a picnic supper and they would go to the park or fishing at the lake. On Sundays they all went to church.

The boy who had everything had noticed that the boy next door went to church on Sundays with his parents. He asked his mom and dad about it, and they said that church was fine for some people, but it wasn't for them.

One Sunday morning, the boy who had everything was playing up in his tree house when he noticed the boy next door getting into the car with his parents. They were all dressed up in their best clothes. He watched as they drove away and when the car was just about out of sight, he hopped on his 10-speed bike and followed them for several blocks down the street and around the corner to their church. He watched from behind a tree as they got out of the car and went into the building. There were a great many other children going into the church with their parents, too. After everyone had gone in, and he could hear music coming from the organ inside the church, he decided that maybe it would be all right if he went in very quietly to see what it was that went on in church.

He tiptoed in. A door was open to a big room where all the people were seated on long benches. He stood behind the door post and watched and listened as the people sang songs, and a man dressed in a white robe and standing on what looked like a little stage with a big lectern, read from a large leather-bound book. Then the man closed the book and talked for a little while. After that he invited everyone to give something he called their offerings. Several people went around with little gold bowls to get all of the offerings. It appeared to the boy that people were putting money in the bowls. When they were finished they took the bowls up to a table in the center of the stage. The man in the white robe went over and uncovered a vase and a loaf of bread. He said some words and then he invited everyone to come up and eat. The little boy was surprised to see that people knelt down before they ate. Watching all of this made him very hungry, and he hoped that they would offer him some of the bread, too.

When everyone was finished, the man in the white robe held up the vase and the bread and asked, "Is there anyone else who would like to come?"

The little boy didn't know what came over him, but he couldn't help himself; he stepped out from behind the door post and called out, "Yes, I would like to come. May I have some?"

The man in the white robe said, "Why, of course you may have some. It is especially for you."

The little boy who had everything went forward and knelt down in front of the man in the white robe. The man broke off a big piece of the bread and showed the little boy how to dip it in the vase. When he put it in his mouth it tasted sweet and satisfying, like nothing he had ever tasted before. And in that moment the little boy felt something change deep down inside himself. He didn't know what it was that was different; he only knew that he wasn't hungry anymore.

Author's Note: The story "Through The Ice" is shared in loving memory of Jessica Vohland, and appears here with the permission of her parents, Robert and Lillian Vohland, and her grandfather, Ernest Vohland.

"The Boy Who Had Everything" first appeared on pages 119-121 of the Cycle B edition of *Lectionary Stories* in 1990. It is printed here with a revised ending. This sermon was delivered at the national convocation of The Fellowship of United Methodists in Worship, Music and the other Arts at Lake Junaluska, North Carolina, on July 18, 1991. An audio version of the sermon was produced and distributed by The United Methodist Publishing House as part of the Circuit Rider Sermon Series.

Apocalypse Children

Happy are those whose help is the God of Jacob, whose hope is in the Lord their God, who made heaven and earth, the sea and all that is in them; who keeps faith forever; who executes justice for the oppressed; who gives food to the hungry. The Lord sets the prisoners free; the Lord opens the eyes of the blind. The Lord lifts up those who are bowed down; the Lord loves the righteous. The Lord watches over the strangers; he upholds the orphan and the widow, but the way of the wicked he brings to ruin.

Psalm 146:5-9

The time is late January, 1991. In a few weeks a ground war will begin in the Persian Gulf.

Here at home, while other children are watching cartoons and playing in backyard sandboxes, a small boy named Scotty is drilling his toy soldiers and watching *Headline News*. He will do nothing else. He keeps the television tuned to CNN all day and all night. His grandparents plead with him to go outside and play with the other children. "You need fresh air and sunshine," they tell him. But he refuses to go. "I have to be ready," he says. Day after day he drills and watches.

Then one day he sees them, his mom and dad, dressed in desert uniforms and looking out at him from the television screen. "We have a son at home," they tell the reporter. "Hi, Scotty," they call out over the airwaves. "We love you. We'll be home soon." Scotty waves at them and they wave back. His mom throws a kiss and his dad salutes. And then the picture fades and Scotty goes outside to play.

Five months later, the war is over. It is the Fourth of July. Scotty, his grandparents, and his dad are seated in a reviewing

106

stand next to the mayor at a victory parade in honor of his mom, who was killed in the war. A Boy Scout troop marches by carrying a large photograph of his mom standing next to her helicopter. She looks young and pretty in her dress uniform. A band follows, playing "God Bless America." Then comes the vice-president, riding in a red convertible with one of the victorious generals. The crowd waves tiny American flags and shouts, "U.S.A., U.S.A." But Scotty does not wave his flag, and he does not join in the cheering. Scotty holds on tightly to his dad's hand and wishes that his mom could come home.

Far away, in a bomb-damaged apartment building in Iraq, a small orphan boy named Abdul is dying for lack of clean water and medicine. Held tightly in his hands is a color photograph of his mom and dad, who were among the 150,000 Iraqis killed in the war. When he dies a few days from now, Abdul will be one of the 170,000 children in Iraq who are expected to die of war-related causes over the next year.

Author's Note: Paragraphs two and three of this story appeared on page 11 in the Cycle C edition of *Lectionary Stories*. The rest of the story was written after the war was over, for a sermon delivered at the national convocation of the Fellowship of United Methodists in Worship, Music and the other Arts at Lake Junaluska, North Carolina, on July 16, 1991. This sermon, titled "The Spirit Way" can be found in Appendix B.

Where Are The Nine?

"And entering a village, he was met by ten people with leprosy, who stood at a distance and lifted up their voices and said, 'Jesus, Teacher, have mercy on us.' And seeing them, Jesus said, 'Go and show yourselves to the priests.' And as they went they were cleansed. Then one of them, seeing that he was healed, turned back praising God with a loud voice; and he fell down at Jesus' feet, giving him thanks. Now that one was a Samaritan. Then said Jesus, 'Were not ten cleansed? Where are the nine?' "
                                                    Luke 17:12-17

Ten soldiers were interviewed by a television reporter before a battle one day. They were allowed to send greetings to their families, and then the reporter asked them to tell how they thought they would react when the fighting began. They all told how well prepared they were, how they would take the fight to the enemy, and how confident they were of victory — that is all but one. He looked into the unblinking eye of the camera and said, "I'm going to keep my head down and try to stay alive."

The fierce battle raged all of that day and most of the night. Thousands of men on both sides were killed or wounded. When the shooting stopped, the television reporter took his crew and looked for the 10 men he had interviewed before the battle. He found the nine confident soldiers cowering in a bunker at the rear, attending to each other's minor wounds. When asked where their friend was, one of them replied, "We don't know. He is probably dead. Our position was overrun by the enemy. We all ran, but he wouldn't come. He said someone had to cover us so we could escape."

Later that day, the television reporter found the 10th soldier in a tent chapel which had been set up next to a field hospital. He was on his knees at the altar giving thanks to God for sparing his life. The reporter could see that the soldier had been seriously wounded, but before he could ask him to tell about the battle the soldier looked up at him and asked, "Have you seen my friends? Are they all right?"

How To Treat Strangers

*When the Son of Man comes in his glory, and all
the angels with him, then he will sit on the throne
of his glory. All the nations will be gathered before
him, and he will separate people from one another
as a shepherd separates the sheep from the goats,
and he will put the sheep at his right hand and the
goats at the left. Then the king will say to those at
his right hand, "Come, you that are blessed by my
Father, inherit the kingdom prepared for you from
the foundation of the world; for I was hungry and
you gave me food, I was thirsty and you gave me
something to drink, I was a stranger and you welcomed me . . ."*

Matthew 25:31-35

Scene I

You live in the country on a quiet, one-lane road. Your
nearest neighbor is almost a mile away. Late one cold, rainy
night, you are wakened by a knock on your door. You peer
through the window, but you do not recognize the person who
is knocking. He or she, you cannot tell which, appears to be
cold and wet. What do you do? Do you open the door? Do
you call the police?

Scene II

You are traveling alone on a quiet country road on a cold,
rainy night. Your car breaks down. You see a house about
a quarter of a mile up the road, and walk toward it. The night

is very dark. You are cold and wet and almost exhausted. You think, "Why did this have to happen to me?" The house is dark, but you decide to risk knocking on the door. A light comes on and a face peers out the window. There is someone at home. You wait for the door to open.

Scene III

Then the righteous will answer him, "Lord when was it that we saw you hungry and gave you food, or thirsty and gave you something to drink? And when was it that we saw you a stranger and welcomed you . . .?" And the king will answer them, "Truly I tell you, just as you did it to one of the least of these who are members of my family, you did it to me."

Matthew 25:37-38, 40

Author's Note: This story is shared in loving memory of June Peichle.

111

The People Of The Eyes

*Who shall ascend the hill of the Lord? And who shall
stand in his holy place? Those who have clean hands
and pure hearts, who do not lift up their souls to
what is false . . .*

Psalm 24:3-4b

Once upon a time, a millenium or two ago, on a volcanic
island that has long since been covered by the waters of the
sea, there existed a small nation known as the People of the
Eyes. The Eyesonians were distinguished by their large round
eyes, and by the fact that they valued seeing clearly more than
anything else. At the center of their city, on the highest hill
overlooking the sea, stood a beautiful temple which had been
carved in the shape of an eyeball. The windows and turrets
of the temple were gilded in gold, and on the pinnacle, which
pointed outward and upward over the sea, was the pupil of
the eye; a large observatory enclosed in dark, tinted glass. Every
day 17 priests in burgundy robes climbed a long, eliptical stair-
case to the center of the eye and took their places in the holy
seers' chairs, where they read the clouds that passed before
them over the waves. Their readings were recorded in the Scroll
of Visions to be read and interpreted by the high priest on Seeing Days. The faithful ascended the hill once every week on
these Seeing Days to pay homage to the All Seeing One, the
Great Eye, who they believed to be the giver of all life. They
passed first through the Hall of Benefactions to lay down their
tithes of silver and gold. Then those who were deemed worthy
— those who had clear seeing eyes and thus pure hearts —
were admitted into the Visionarium to offer prayers to the All
Seeing One and to listen as the high priest read from the Scroll
of Visions.

Ironically, the persons with the most status and power in this society that valued seeing clearly above all things, were those who had just one eye. Only the One-Eyes were permitted to be priests, political leaders, healers, teachers and merchants. It was believed that they possessed a clarity of vision unequalled by persons who had two eyes or three eyes.

Two-eyed people worked in lower level jobs in the fishing fleet, in the marketplace and as managers of the households of their one-eyed masters. They were given no formal education and could not vote in the elections, but were allowed to enter the temple and to offer their prayers from a roped off section in the back of the Visionarium.

Three-eyed persons, who made up only about 10 percent of the population, were considered to be unclean: an abomination in the eye of the deity, and unfit to enter the temple on any occasion. Their extra eye was believed to distort their vision, preventing them from seeing clearly. The Two-Eyes lorded over them and forced them to do the most menial and undesirable tasks. They were shunned altogether by the One-Eyes. Marriage was forbidden to them and according to a strictly enforced law, they were not to look a two-eyed person or a one-eyed person in the eye. Any group of three one-eyed persons, or six two-eyed persons, could, upon the word of a single witness, have a three-eyed person's face put out for as much as glancing at their better's face. There were hundreds of three-eyed persons who had suffered this miserable fate. They made their living by begging outside the gates of the temple on Seeing Days.

This cruel three-tiered caste system grew harsher with each passing year. Whenever a three-eyed baby was born — always to two-eyed or one-eyed parents, because three-eyed persons were not allowed to give birth — a day of mourning was declared, and the child was taken to a sanitarium on the edge of the island to be raised and schooled in the ways of his or her own kind. Some parents resisted this forced parting and managed to keep their three-eyed children for a time, but the authorities always found them out. Then the parents were taken in chains before the high priest to be admonished. "You are not seeing clearly," he would say. "Our ways are the will of the Great Eye. The All Seeing One's words are written in the Scroll of Visions. Let all eyes be open to the truth of the way." So the oppression and the persecution went on for centuries, until one day there came a new vision.

A young priest was reading the clouds that day from his perch in the pupil-shaped observatory, on the pinnacle of the temple, when he happened to see a most unusual formation passing before him. A large, dark cloud, which appeared to have three eyes, was swallowing up two smaller clouds. One of the smaller clouds had one eye and the other had two eyes. After a time, the three clouds separated and floated along together, equal in size, until they disappeared over the horizon. When the young priest reported his most unusual sighting to the other priests they agreed that the message was unmistakably clear. He was about to record what he had seen in the School of Visions when the high priest intervened, saying, "I cannot deliver a message like that to the people. It is more than they will be able to accept. They will not believe it is from the All Seeing One. Many of them will be angry with us and they will stop coming to the temple on Seeing Days. How will we operate the temple without their tithes of silver and gold. Surely the All Seeing One would not want us to read a vision from the Scroll that would cause our people to turn away."

"But what, then, shall we record in the Scroll of Visions?" one of the youngest priests inquired.

"We shall say that there was no new vision this week, and I shall simply read one of the old visions as I have often done in the past when no new vision was given. When the time is right, when the people are ready, then we shall share this new vision with them."

So the new vision was not recorded in the Scroll of Visions.

On the very next Seeing Day, just as the high priest stood up to read from the scroll, the temple was struck by a bolt of lightning which shattered the glass in the pupil observatory, high above the Visionarium where the worshipers were seated.

A single shard of the broken glass fell straight down into the center of the Visionarium, piercing the heart of the high priest, and he fell down dead. All of the people, including the 16 remaining priests, were terrified. No one moved and not a word was spoken for several moments. At last one of the younger priests, the one who had sighted the startling cloud formation, stepped forward. "Be calm. Have no fear," he said as he looked out on the frightened worshipers. "We have a new vision to share with you. We had planned to keep it from you until a later time, but now it is clear that we cannot hide what the All Seeing One wishes for you to see." Then he told them exactly what he had seen in the clouds and announced that three-eyed, two-eyed and one-eyed people should all be considered equal, as it had been declared by the Great Eye. In the same moment the eyes of the three-eyed blind beggars outside of the temple gates were healed, and they rushed into the Visionarium, fell on their knees and began to give thanks to the All Seeing One for their deliverance.

From that day on, everyone among the People of the Eyes saw clearly and lived in peace and harmony together.

Appendix B

The Spirit Way

The following narrative sermon was preached at the convocation of The Fellowship of United Methodists In Music, Worship and The Other Arts at Lake Junaluska, North Carolina, July 17, 1991. It includes three stories: "Old Farmer" which first appeared on pages 19-23 of Lectionary Stories For Cycle B, *"Apocalypse Children" which is found on pages 106-107 of this volume and "Out Of The Water," also from the Cycle B book, pages 44-47.*

"Do not let your hearts be troubled. Believe in God, believe also in me. In my Father's house there are many dwelling places. If it were not so, would I have told you that I go to prepare a place for you? And if I go and prepare a place for you, I will come again and will take you to myself, so that where I am, there you may be also.

"I did not say these things to you from the beginning, because I was with you. But now I am going to him who sent me; yet none of you ask me, 'Where are you going?' But because I have said these things to you, sorrow has filled your hearts. Nevertheless, I tell you the truth: it is to your advantage that I go away, for if I do not go away, the Advocate will not come to you; but if I go, I will send him to you. And when he comes, he will prove the world wrong about sin and righteousness and judgment: about sin, because they do not believe in me; about righteousness, because I am going to the Father and you will see me no longer; about judgment, because the ruler of this world has been condemned. I still have many things to say to you, but you cannot bear them now. When the Spirit of truth comes, he will guide you into all truth . . . ."

John 14:1-3, 16:4b-13a.

In the hills of southwest Wisconsin, in the little community of Willow Bluff, they tell this story about an old farmer by the name of Alfie Georgeson. I say old farmer because that's what everyone called him, "Old Farmer."

The nickname originated one day during a bull session down at the filling station. It was what one might call a community christening. Some of the guys from the cheese factory were sitting around the cooler having a pop after work. Alfie walked in looking like he always looked when he came into town. Junior Ridley took one look at him and said, "Alfie, you look like the original old farmer."

It was true. Alfie was never seen wearing anything but the uniform of his chosen profession — bib overalls. He had three pairs; one good striped pair which he wore only when he went into town, and two faded blue pairs which he wore for everyday. One was for wearing while the other was in the wash. The rest of the uniform was standard issue at any farm supply store; a blue cotton work shirt, triple hook work boots and Co-op hat. That was the old farmer.

The name stuck. After a while people began to say it to his face. "Hey, Old Farmer, how are you doing?" Alfie didn't mind. That's how he thought of himself, too.

Alfie loved the land. He owned 80 acres of bottom land, all tillable, which he farmed with a pair of Percheron horses. Alfie said they were the best work horses in the country, and there wasn't anyone around who would dispute it. Everybody else farmed with tractors. If they had work horses they were only for show or maybe for pulling at the county fair.

Alfie's horses were for working. They had been pulling together for 20 years. They were like old friends. It wasn't that he was against motor propelled machinery. He just never saw the need for it. The farm was paid for, it provided he and Elizabeth with a modest but adequate living, and the horses were able to do all of the pulling work that needed to be done. The rest Alfie did by hand. He preferred it that way.

Long days were a way of life on the farm. Alfie's alarm clock went off precisely at four-thirty every morning. He went straight to the barn, fed and watered the livestock, cleaned the stalls, harnessed the horses, spread the manure, fed the chickens and gathered the eggs. He was usually back at the house for breakfast by seven, and off to the fields by seven-thirty.

Field work was done at the horses' pace. When they tired, Alfie rested with them until they were ready to pull again. The end of the day came when the horses had had enough. Alfie never pushed them beyond their endurance, even when he was in a hurry to get something done. There would always be another day. They were usually back in the barn by five: five-thirty at the latest.

The unharnessing was Alfie's favorite part of the day. The ritual had an almost sacramental quality for him. The horses always appreciated the rub down, something they communicated to him in subtle ways that only an old farmer would understand. This and the warm aromas that filled the stalls, a combination of lathered leather, fresh hay, oats in the manger and the pungent odor of the remains of same in the gutter under each horse's tail, made him feel that all was right with the world. Fresh country air, city folks kind of turned up their noses. But to an old farmer it is a sign of God's presence.

Elizabeth never got used to the fact that he brought these smells with him when he came into the house, although after 60 years she had learned to accept it as one of the givens of farm life. She had been a city girl, if you can call a town of 1,600 a city, the daughter of the banker no less. Alfie always said she'd never done a lick of work in her life till she came to the farm. It wasn't true, of course, but Alfie liked to tease her about it just the same. Elizabeth loved Alfie. "My dear old farmer," she used to say when she talked about him with her close friends. She would have been perfectly content if only he would have gone to church with her once in a while. Once or twice a year would have been enough, but he would never go.

It wasn't that Alfie didn't love God. Elizabeth knew that his communication with the Creator was continual. It was part of the rhythm of his life, not in any formal way, of course; they never said grace before meals except on a few occasions when a preacher came to visit; but she knew that God was always in his thoughts as he worked the land. He said so once and she knew it was so because she could see it in his face as she watched him work. It was probably just that he didn't like crowds. Alfie didn't feel comfortable when there were a lot of people around so he never went anywhere there was going to be a crowd.

He would have liked to have gone for Elizabeth's sake, had almost brought himself to do it on several occasions, but after all those years of not going it would have been an event. He didn't think he could take all the smiles and self-satisfied looks as people congratulated him and patted him on the back. He knew what they would be thinking. "It's good to see you in church, you old goat! It's about time. Where have you been all of these years?" So he could never bring himself to go, even for Elizabeth's sake. It was a weakness, he knew, but he had never been able to overcome it.

There had been only one exception to this long-standing rule and Elizabeth never forgot it. It happened on a Christmas Eve. Elizabeth sang in the choir and when she looked out that particular night just as the service was about to begin she couldn't believe her eyes. There was Alfie sitting in the back row of their little church with the five Enderman kids. He had on his good striped overalls and he looked terribly uncomfortable, but there he was.

Elizabeth found out later why he was there. He told her the kids brought him, but it had been the other way around.

The Enderman family lived about a quarter of a mile up the road. They were only three for about a year. Their dad drank and could never hold a job for long, so the family moved around from one rundown farm house to another. But while they were there the kids came over regularly to see Alfie and Elizabeth. They would talk to Alfie while he worked in the barn and sometimes he would give them a ride in the haywagon. Then they would all go up to the house and Elizabeth would get out the milk and cookies.

That Christmas Eve Elizabeth left early to rehearse with the choir before the service. When the kids came over Alfie discovered that they knew very little about Christmas. They didn't have a Christmas tree; they didn't expect many presents, and they knew nothing about the birth of Jesus. It didn't seem right to Alfie that any child should grow up without hearing the Christmas story. So he hitched up the horses (Elizabeth had the car), threw some blankets and hay in the back of a wagon, packed the kids in and brought them to church.

Elizabeth learned all of this when they took a tree and the presents over to their house the next day.

After that Elizabeth picked up the Enderman kids and took them to church every Sunday. She even got their mom to go once in a while. But once had been enough for Alfie. He never went back.

On Sunday mornings while Elizabeth was in church, Alfie would curry the horses and catch up on little odd jobs around the barn. He spent most of his leisure time in the barn. That was just where he wanted to be. And that was where Elizabeth found him that Sunday morning after church. She went to the house first, as she always did, and she didn't go to look for him until long after lunch was ready and she realized he hadn't come in to wash up at the usual time. She found him propped up against a bale of hay. He looked like he always looked when he fell asleep in the easy chair after supper. The doctor told her later that his heart just gave out, said he was surprised that he was able to go on as long as he had.

The church was full on the day of the funeral. Everybody loved "Old Farmer." Elizabeth didn't remember much of what was said. She did remember the fuss everyone made about the horses. She saw to it that Alfie's casket was placed on a hay wagon and drawn to the cemetery by his beloved Percherons. Everybody said it was just the right touch.

And she remembered the preacher reading the familiar words from John:

In my Father's house there are many dwelling places. If it were not so, would I have told that I go to prepare a

place for you? And if I go and prepare a place for you,
I will come again and take you to myself, so that where
I am, you may be also. And you know the way to the
place where I am going.

She repeated the words in her mind over and over again as she tried in vain to sleep that night. Did Alfie know the way? Could Christ in his infinite mercy make a place for him, too?

The Spirit lives and works in us in ways that are wondrous and perplexing. The Spirit, Jesus declares, ". . . will prove the world wrong about sin and righteousness and judgment."

Is it possible that we have been wrong about sin and righteousness and judgment?

Go back in time with me to January of 1991. In a few weeks a ground war will begin in the Persian Gulf.

Here at home, while other children are watching cartoons and playing in backyard sandboxes, a small boy named Scotty is drilling his toy soldiers and watching *Headline News.* He will do nothing else. He keeps the television tuned to CNN all day and all night. His grandparents plead with him to go outside and play with the other children. "You need fresh air and sunshine," they tell him. But he refuses to go. "I have to be ready," he says. Day after day he drills and watches.

Then one day he sees them, his mom and dad, dressed in desert uniforms and looking out at him from the television screen. "We have a son at home," they tell the reporter. "Hi, Scotty," they call out over the airwaves. "We love you. We'll be back home soon." Scotty waves at them and they wave back. His mom throws him a kiss and his dad salutes. And then the picture fades and Scotty goes outside to play.

Five months later, the war is over. It is the Fourth of July. Scotty, his grandparents, and his dad are seated in a reviewing stand next to the mayor at a victory parade in honor of his mom, who was killed in the war. A Boy Scout troop marches by carrying a large photograph of his mom standing next to her helicopter. She lookes young and pretty in her dress uniform. A band follows, playing "God Bless America." Then comes the vice-president, riding in a red convertible with one of the victorious generals. The crowd waves tiny American flags and shouts, "U.S.A., U.S.A." But Scotty does not wave his flag, and he does not join in the cheering. Scotty holds on tightly to his dad's hand and wishes that his mom would come home.

Far away, in a bomb-damaged apartment building in Iraq, a small orphan boy named Abdul is dying for lack of clean water and medicine. Held tightly in his hands is a color photograph of his mom and dad, who were among the estimated 150,000 Iraquis killed in the war. When he dies a few days from now, Abdul will be one of the 17,000 children in Iraq who are expected to die of war-related causes over the next year.

However one feels about the rightness or wrongness of the Persian Gulf War, there is cause for lamentation. We citizens of the planet Earth have just participated in an horrendous slaughter of over 100,000 people. We may never know for sure how many have died from our smart bombs and their deadly scud missiles. The Iraquis blame us for the slaughter and we blame them. How can any of us live with what has been done — with the human suffering and damage to the environment that will last for generations? Is it possible that we have all been wrong about sin and righteousness and judgment?

Is it possible for all of us sinners — Iraquis and Americans who have strayed so far from the Spirit — to be forgiven and reconciled with the one who gives us our lives? Can Christ in his infinite mercy make a place for us, too?

The Spirit way is not our way, but Jesus assures us that the Spirit will guide us ". . . into all truth . . ."

Elsie Dewitt was upset when she came into the sanctuary. She wasn't able to sit in her usual place near the middle of the pew. The Murphys usually saved it for her, but they were out of town today, and there were several visitors in their places. Elsie had to sit near the end of the pew, next to the center aisle. She didn't like to sit next to the aisle. That was where her late husband had always sat. But that wasn't the only reason she was upset. It was the second Sunday of the month, baptism Sunday. She could see at least three families with babies sitting near the front, not far from the baptismal font. No doubt the visitors in her pew were relatives of one of these families.

Elsie had to force herself to come to church on baptism Sundays. She came partly because she didn't know how she could explain to her friends why she didn't want to come, but mostly because she could never justify not going to worship. Elsie had been raised to believe that the Lord's day belonged to God. She always went to worship on Sunday. She wouldn't miss for any reason. Any other Sunday she would have been glad to have been there. Worship was a joy for her. Elsie had never thought of it as a duty. But baptism Sundays were different. They were something she suffered, like one might endure the occasional migraine headache. She viewed it as part of her lot in life.

The reason was a secret that she had shared with no one, not even her late husband. Her parents had known, of course, but they were long gone.

Midway through the service, Elsie's heart skipped a beat. The pastor was headed her way, carrying one of the babies she had just baptized. It was a custom in the church for the pastor to give each baptized baby to someone in the congregation to hold during the baptismal prayer, as a way of welcoming him or her into the family of God. "It couldn't be. Oh no!" Elsie thought, as the pastor smiled at her and handed her the baby. One of her greatest fears had been realized. Now what was she going to do? She couldn't just hand the baby back to the pastor and ask her to give him to someone else.

The child deserved better than that on this important day. But it wasn't right, it just wasn't right. She, who had failed in her duty to her own child, had no business holding the child of another during the consummation of a sacrament.

Elsie bit her lip and hung on to the baby, trying hard not to let her discomfort show. She breathed a sigh of relief when, at last, the pastor finished the prayer and took the baby back to his parents. The worst was over. But how could she ever forgive herself for allowing it to happen? Elsie waited in agony for the next standing hymn. Then she got up quietly and left the church.

That afternoon Elsie called the pastor and asked if she could see her at her earliest convenience. She was determined to relieve herself of the burden of the terrible secret she had carried alone for all of these years. Elsie knew that if she didn't share it now, she would carry it with her into eternity.

Pastor Carol agreed to see her at two o'clock the next afternoon. Elsie arrived promptly at the appointed hour. She looked pale, and her eyes were swollen and red. "I couldn't sleep at all last night," she told Pastor Carol. "I've been deeply troubled ever since the baptisms yesterday. You may have noticed that I left the service early."

"I did see you go," Pastor Carol said, "and I'm glad you've come to talk about it."

"I'll have to start at the very beginning," Elsie said. And then she poured it all out. "I had a child out of wedlock when I was 16. My folks kept me home from school as soon as they found out I was expecting. Dad simply told the teacher that I was needed on the farm. In those days that was a common occurrence, so no one thought anything about it. And no one ever found out about the baby. My mother assisted me in the delivery. That went well, but the baby was small, and he had difficulty breathing from the first day. I knew I should have sent for the pastor and had him baptized, but I was afraid of what he might say. So we never sent for him. The baby died two weeks after he was born. We buried him in the family cemetery on the ridge behind the house. I have never been

124

able to tell anyone about my failure to have him baptized. I tried to put it out of my mind, but every time I see a baby baptized in church, I remember, and I wonder if my baby is all right. I can't imagine that God would keep him out of heaven just because he hadn't been baptized, but I don't know. I worry about it, and even more now that I'm older.

Then Elsie broke down and wept. Pastor Carol got up, put her arms around her and held her for a long time.

The next Sunday morning after the sermon, Pastor Carol announced that Elsie had something she wanted to share with everyone. Elsie got up from where she was sitting in her usual pew, walked hesitantly all the way up the aisle, then turned and stood facing the congregation about three feet in front of the baptismal font. Pastor Carol handed her the microphone. Elsie took a deep breath, and then she told them the whole story, just as she had related it in the pastor's office. When she was finished Pastor Carol took the cover off the baptismal font and invited everyone in the congregation to join hands as they prayed. And then, calling Elsie's long lost child by name, she commended him to God. Then she prayed the prayer of thanksgiving over the water: "Pour out your Holy Spirit, to bless this gift of water and those who receive it, to wash away their sin and clothe them in righteousness throughout their lives, that dying and being raised with Christ, they may share in his final victory."

When the prayer was finished, Pastor Carol invited the congregation to come forward and dip their hands into the water and remember their baptisms. They all came. Elsie was the last to come. Her hands trembled as she lifted them up out of the water. Somewhere from deep inside herself she heard a voice saying that all was well.

Author's Note: The complete prayer of Thanksgiving Over the Water can be found on pages 41 and 42 of *The United Methodist Hymnal.*

Afterword

By Jo Perry-Sumwalt

How I Write And Edit Stories

Writing is a very personal, individualized activity. No two people approach it in exactly the same way. Some writers need a particular atmosphere to work in, and some can find inspiration anywhere. Some writers compose their ideas at a typewriter or computer, and others, like me, prefer to hand-write the first draft. I find the words flow better from my brain through a pen than through my fingertips on a keyboard. But I have found, through study and experience, that there are a number of helpful guidelines to follow.

Since inspiration is such a key element of writing, writer's block is an annoying frustration. Brainstorming and free-writing can loosen tension and provide topics. I have learned to make lists of people I've known, places I've been, character types, observations, experiences and contemporary social problems for possible subject matter. John keeps journals of daily thoughts, inspirations and personal experiences for future material. He also draws on newspaper and magazine articles, family history and ready-made sources, like lectionary scriptures. In my experience, once the plot and/or characters have begun to form, free-writing may give me direction.

Free-writing is an exercise in which the writer puts into words, with no regard to form or order, any and all thoughts pertaining to the subject at hand. If I have a main character in mind, but no plot for a story, I try writing down all of the details about that character that come to me. I use my imagination and fill a page. When I read over what I have written, I look for patterns of behavior or quirky characteristics which might provide or fill out the plot of the story. Then I eliminate any information that seems unimportant. Not every thought is viable, let alone golden. Although it's not easy to do, I try to be my own toughest critic.

Editing and critiquing one's own writing is a difficult process. Since the words and phrasings come from within, our own reading of them may not expose problems like spelling errors, misused punctuation poor word choices and sentence structure, and use of cliches. When I go over John's stories or my own, I look for all of these things. I read the phrasings carefully and try to be aware of lines that seem stilted or hard to understand. I recommend that writers who seriously intend to seek publication read books and manuals on the mechanics of writing. Know and understand sentence structure, punctuation and spelling. I love to play with words. Their order and usage can be an exciting challenge, and finding just the right combinations is a reward itself. However, I try not to fall into the trap of using big, impressive words where a small, ordinary word would do. Simplicity and directness are desirable qualities. And if writers are unsure of their abilities, I highly recommend taking a class.

Many technical schools, colleges and universities offer creative writing classes. Take one! I found that it forced me to keep writing, to dig deeper into my own thoughts, emotions and abilities, and to learn to share my work with others. It also put me in contact with other aspiring writers who needed support and feedback. If there is no college or technical school nearby, seek out other people with an interest in writing and form your own writing support group. Give yourself writing assignments, or agree on the number of creative pieces you will share with the group during a given number of meetings. For me, critiquing helped develop my own skills while attempting to aid the other writer. Local libraries carry resource materials on writing, word mechanics and structure and might even prove to be a meeting place if they have rooms that can be reserved. The object of a writing group is not to rip one another's work apart, but to give constructive criticism. I had to learn not to be so possessive of my own writing that I rejected another's suggestions. Every writer is defensive of his or her work. It is a part of us, and its creation is a birthing process; naturally its reception or rejection is taken personally.

But, if we are so protective that we cannot hear criticism, our work will never improve. I try to balance what can be changed without compromising the integrity of my work — what can be eliminated or altered to strengthen it — with what must be left as it is. It is a judgment call from within.

Each author must follow his or her own intuition; that is what keeps literature exciting. There are no absolutes to writing successful stories. But I recommend becoming knowledgeable about the conventions of writing that are the guidelines for publication. When an author finds his or her own voice and applies the necessary conventions, resulting stories become a joy not only to the writer, but to the readers whose hearts and minds they will reach.